EVERY CHILD – A CHANCE TO CHOOSE

Every Child –
A Chance to
Choose

PENNY FRANK

EASTBOURNE

First published 2002

ISBN 1 84291 053 1

*Cartoons in text are
by Mark Cripps*

Published by
KINGSWAY COMMUNICATIONS LTD
Lottbridge Drove, Eastbourne, BN23 6NT, England.
Email: books@kingsway.co.uk

Book design and production for the publishers by
Bookprint Creative Services, P.O. Box 827, BN21 3YJ, England.
Printed in Great Britain.

In memory of my parents,
Lawrence and Muriel Iles,
and in faith for our grandson,
Stephen Timothy,
'from generation to generation'.

Contents

CONTENTS

Foreword

As the great west doors of Liverpool Cathedral opened to welcome me as Bishop of Liverpool, the lone figure of a child stood to speak the first words: 'Bishop James, remember what Jesus said: "Truly I tell you, whoever does not receive the kingdom of God like a child will never enter it."'

Those words echoed around the vast sacred space filled with people of all ages, as a child led us in the worship of God. They have become a seal of my ministry. I long (and that is not an exaggeration) for the church to embrace children with the same determination as Jesus, who sternly resisted those adults who wanted to shoo them away. He took them to himself, assuring them of a place in his kingdom as well as his arms.

Ever since becoming a bishop, whenever I visit a parish I send a form to ask specifically if they would like me to address any children present. The request requires crossing out a simple 'yes' or 'no'. Sometimes the 'yes' is scrubbed out with such vigour I wonder about the feelings towards children that lie behind the action.

I commend this book by Penny Frank not because I am President of CPAS, nor because I have long been an admirer of her work, but because I believe these pages might help us all to dig beneath our actions and feelings to ask why we are still excluding so many children from the body of Christ.

In his novel *The Power and the Glory* Graham Greene wrote, 'There's a moment in childhood when the door opens and lets the future in.' The lintels of that door include parents' behaviour, public policies and church attitudes.

The gospel begins not just with the demonstration that God himself could become a child, but with the story of how vulnerable children are before adults who seek to exclude them. Herod's destruction of innocent children reminds us that there are still in today's world sinister forces that threaten the future of our children. You will remember those haunting words of Jesus: 'And if anyone causes one of these little ones who believe in me to sin, it would be better for him to be thrown into the sea with a large millstone tied around his neck' (Mark 9:42).

These episodes and sayings may seem dramatic, but they are there to disturb our complacency. I hope that you will be challenged to read on for the sake of the children.

The Rt. Revd James Jones
Bishop of Liverpool

Introduction

Given the choice, which would you rather hear first: the good news or the bad news? Do you find yourself describing a glass as 'half-empty' or 'half-full'? You hear an adult cautioning a child to walk on the pavement, rather than risk wandering onto the busy carriageway. Do you think she's a 'voice of doom and gloom', or do you silently applaud her for caring enough about the child's safety to speak out?

This book is all about giving every child – and I mean *every* child – the opportunity to discover Jesus and to respond to him. In other words, it's about giving children the chance to choose.

There is good news between every chapter in this book. I've gathered ten 'Storyboxes', each one giving a mini-picture of good work with children going on up and down the country. They come from people who have looked at the multitude of children living near their church and have cared enough to tell them about Jesus and God's love. They are stories that could be repeated by all sorts of people from all sorts of churches around the British Isles. In the face of such good news we need to celebrate and give God the glory for it.

What about bad news? Yes, there is some. I think we ought to hear about that too. The psalm writer says that the people of God are not afraid of hearing bad news (Psalm 112:7). Nothing is impossible for God to change. But we need to face up to the bad news so that God can bring change through us. With this in mind, my book has five main aims.

1. Faith in God's timeless promises. I want people to finish the book feeling concern for the issues about which I feel shame and feeling excited about the good things too. But above all I want us to trust in the big promises of God, which stand for all time.

2. A picture of now. I try to make a sketch of children's evangelism in the British Isles at the beginning of the twenty-first century. It is only a sketch, but I try to put this into the context of what is going on in both the church and society. I want to make connections so that the basis for my arguments is understandable.

3. Identifying problems. In pointing out what I believe are some key problems, I am not trying to apportion blame. Rather, I am calling for change from those who are in a position of power to make change possible. When I look at the

statistics showing the increasing 'rate of loss' of children from the church during my lifetime, I feel ashamed. I began my ministry with children when I was thirteen – that's forty-three years ago. In those years the church has bled, haemorrhaging children. I am in no position to point the finger. I am simply broken-hearted at what I see around me, as my work for the Church Pastoral Aid Society takes me all over the country.

4. Taking responsibility. I want all of us to own the problem as *our* responsibility. Maybe our local church has thriving children's work; perhaps we are thrilled at what God is doing through us with children. But I would still like us each to pause where we are and, for a moment, look further afield. I beg you to consider that the way things are going in your church may not be typical of the British Isles as a whole. I would like each reader to be willing to get involved in some way in bringing children's evangelism across the land into a 'better place before God'. Our society is concerned about human rights. That's good. My book offers the challenge: how can we express genuine concern for the rights of children if we ignore their basic right to their Christian inheritance?

5. A chance to choose. In calling for every child to have the chance to choose Jesus, I am not campaigning for high-pressure missions or indoctrination programmes. I simply want children to hear the Christian good news in the way that most helps them to understand and absorb it. I don't want them put in a position of dilemma and anxiety. But I do

want them to go through their lives knowing how to have an everlasting relationship with God that will enable them to achieve their full potential as human beings.

Using this book

I want to set people thinking. I hope to get them talking, questioning, imagining and praying. Above all I want this book to encourage leaders and members of local churches to take action.

So please use this book as a resource. If you are reading it on your own, why not make a list of two or three people in your church with whom you'd like to discuss the key points? Alternatively, why not gather a group of concerned people and work through the book as a way of reviewing all that your church does and could do regarding evangelism with children?

At the end of each chapter there is 'Talk about it' – a short list of provocative discussion-starters. You can continue these discussions, or start new ones, by logging on to this book's website: www.chancetochoose.com

In acknowledgement ...

I am proud to work within an organisation that has released me from other responsibilities for three years because of this concern for children. That concern has also been endorsed through the specific funding that has made the work possible – from trusts, churches and individuals.

As you read on, you may be tempted to call me obsessed or extreme. You may feel some sympathy for those who live or work with me. They certainly deserve more gratitude than I can possibly put into words. My thanks go to my colleagues James Lawrence and Rory Keegan. Without them, my concern and passion about children's evangelism could easily have lost its way. They have supplied an endless flow of encouragement, humour and common sense.

I'm grateful to Dave Roberts and Sue Price of Kingsway for their support and encouragement.

My husband Tom has, through more than thirty years, freed me to be involved in evangelism with children, often at great personal cost. He is my relational rock and provides shelter for me from the storms.

Fasten your seatbelts . . .

And, of course, there are storms! Bishop Gavin Reid, my mentor through some of the last fifteen years, sums up the situation like this:

Of course things have gone wrong and a crucial call (I believe from God) has not been acted upon. What we need to see is WHY it hasn't been acted upon and the criticisms have to be positive in relation to the real reasons. I see these to be:

- the whole gap between talkers and the people who must make things happen;
- the inability of the church to prioritise, especially when it means dropping things to take on the new;

- the deep-seated unawareness of the true significance of work among children, be it pastoral or evangelistic;
- the self-centred spirituality that pervades our churches where things are driven by the perceived needs of those who are already inside;
- theological hang-ups about evangelism in general and the true nature of the gospel.

So, for the good news as well as the bad, I beg you to read on.

Penny Frank

1. Wonderful World?

Setting the scene for children

'And I think to myself: what a wonderful world . . . oh yeees!' sang Louis Armstrong. And it certainly is a wonderful world for many children in the British Isles today. It is as though they grow up with access to everything they could wish for: colour, activity, real or virtual company, sport, instant food and instant entertainment. For many of them there are overseas holidays and fashionable clothes as well.

Wonderful – for some

For some of them everything is paid for with a plastic card and there is little experience of handling coins. They are confident about buying over the Internet, and have few problems with transport, since caring parents ferry them through their busy social diaries. In a world that offers a plethora of entertainment, boredom is the main threat for many children. Their imaginations become satiated with ever more startling special effects in their video games and movies.

In many areas we could certainly make a strong argument for the world of the child never having been more wonderful than it is today. Of course, those who work among children at the edges of society would be quick to point out that this is only true of the privileged few. They would want us to remember the increasing number of children who live below the poverty line and rarely have enough nutritious food to eat. These children, who begin life with the odds so stacked against them, will rarely be able to better themselves, socially or educationally.

The Child Poverty Action Group, and other agencies that campaign tirelessly on behalf of the poor, would want us to be aware that the world is far from wonderful for a rising tide of children and their carers. They remind us that over the last generation, while many have become richer, the poor have become poorer. For example, the average income of the poorest fifth of UK households grew at an average annual rate of 1.4 per cent in the three years to 2000. During the same period the average income of the richest fifth increased by 2.8 per cent a year.[1]

The Viva Network is an international 'family of networks' set up to link Christians working with 'children at risk' worldwide. In his book *Reaching Children in Need* (Kingsway Publications), Director Patrick McDonald identifies the

---

[1] *The Structure of Welfare* (Institute of Fiscal Studies, May 2001).

growing number of children in the UK who are living below the poverty line.

Nor is it simply wealth and poverty that divide. So too do war and peace. A representative of the Diocese of London says:

> In some [of our] schools, one only has to walk through the door and meet the children, to know which part of the world is at war this week. In those schools there are children who do not speak English, who have been traumatised by what they have witnessed, who have experienced real suffering. . . .[2]

Within our own shores we have children who have grown up with such fear and trauma – it comes from within the UK and without. It is a far-reaching influence on many children.

The context for children's evangelism in the modern UK is very different from that of the 1950s when I first became involved. For the rich and for the poor, the northerner and the southerner, those at peace and those affected by war, the world has radically changed, whether people would describe it as wonderful or not.

A universal right

In the language of our time, each individual has rights. Our culture accepts that basic rights include warmth, food,

---

[2] *Way Ahead – Church of England Schools in the New Millennium* (Church House Publishing, 2001).

shelter, clean water, human contact and education. Some of these rights seem purely physical, but all of them make a difference not only to the outward comfort of a person but also to how they think and feel. The National Curriculum for England and Wales acknowledges 'the spiritual' in its statement of values: 'We value ourselves as unique human beings capable of spiritual, moral, intellectual and physical growth and development.'[3]

The gospel of Jesus Christ is the rightful inheritance of every child. Long ago people in this country campaigned for the basic rights of children. But as well as arguing for their right to drink clean water or to learn to read, they cared for their spiritual welfare. When we withhold spiritual information from children, we threaten their rights. We leave those who are vulnerable in a place of spiritual risk.

Every child has the right to hear the information that would give her or him the chance to choose Jesus. Without information children cannot make up their own minds. Yet today in the UK, children are unlikely to hear the gospel of Jesus properly explained even *once* during their childhood.

This book sets out to look at this crisis and it challenges Christians to reintroduce Christianity to childhood. It has been written in the firm belief that there is a crisis to face and that answers do exist. It argues that meeting this challenge is not simply a possibility, but a biblical imperative.

---

[3] National Curriculum Online, www.nc.uk.net

Today's 'wonderful' world

Naturally evangelism among modern children will need to take on the colours and flavour of their world if it is to be effective. We cannot find out how to hand on the faith to children unless we know what childhood is like today. We need to be in touch with children's likes and dislikes, their concerns, their dreams, what makes them tick.

We need to be in touch with children's likes and dislikes.

What is the world of the child like at the beginning of this century? Is it even possible to begin to describe it when there is such disparity between the childhood experience of the rich and the poor, those living with conflict and those in peace? Here is a small range of 'snapshots' which I hope will give us a taste of their world – wherever they live in the British Isles and whoever they are.

Stimulation

The child's world today is full of colour and activity. Psychedelic graphics shout at them from every screen and hoarding. Clothes, books, magazines, videos, interactive TV, the Net – everything clamours for their attention with colour and movement. Our children have been born into this kind of wonderful world and their attention is educated for this kind of stimulation. Whether they are rich or poor, whatever their intellect or surroundings, they are not attracted to that which is monochrome. Their preference is for entertainment that is fast moving and varied, changing its approach or scene in seconds, where the conversation or commentary is almost coded in its economy.

Marketing and merchandise

Children are the targets for new marketing ploys. Granada Television's Head of Sponsorship and Licensing, Martin Lowde, says: 'We're putting increased emphasis on the eight to twelves as a group, largely because of interest from advertisers and toy manufacturers.'[4] The article continues: '[satellite TV company] Nickelodeon's 5–7pm slot has audiences aged seven to twelve as high as 200,000. Advertisers including Gap and Boots' Glitter Babe have targeted this spot.'

---

[4] *The Independent*, 29 May 2001.

The era of 'tweenagers' (pre-teens with spending power) is with us. For this important age group, playground credibility is everything. Parents are often as susceptible as their offspring. They see in their children's aspirations the means of proving themselves as providers.

Among younger children it is often the parent who makes the first move. It was parents who, a few years ago, came to blows in the big stores at Christmas when the must-have Teletubbies merchandise ran out. New, young parents are easy prey for manufacturers, whose products are presented as having the power to make their children bright, confident and attractive.

The marketers increasingly offer products that make the child into a little adult – clothes and belongings give the small child a grown-up appearance that is apparently attractive first to the parent and later to the child. It seems that childhood is shrinking with each new generation. Parents will be tempted to buy any product that gives their child the lead over others, or presents them as sophisticated or advanced.

Toddlers are often bewildered with their choice of toys, even at a stage when playthings like wooden spoons, baking tins and packaging seem more fascinating than shop-bought toys. Yet the provision for these children in toy stores is overwhelming.

For school-age children, the Pokémon phenomenon has been startling. Schools have often refused to allow the Pokémon cards onto the premises because of fights and arguments caused by the bartering and exchange. Other related merchandise has poured into the stores, offering clothes, bedding, books, stationery, shoes and, of course, the obligatory video games. If this craze has left your life untouched, take this opportunity to visit one of the Pokémon websites and browse through this huge industry (www.pokemon.com).

Spirituality

Children are spiritual people. This truth has been recognised by those in the world of entertainment. Look through the cartoons, films and videos being promoted for children and you will find a world of spirits, ghosts, magic and witches. Children's literature has always drawn on the world of the unseen for its themes of mystery and adventure, but this is now almost exclusively the case. The world of Harry Potter has challenged every adult Christian to read and consider exactly what is being offered to our children as 'normal' spirituality.

Virtual reality

Another snapshot in our childhood scene must be of the world where the computer and television provide dependable, 'virtual' relationships. Children are confident with computers. They have never known the world without them. They know how reliable and logical they are. They know that a computer does not have a 'bad day'. Unlike human relationships, circumstances do not turn a machine into a human threat.

The child sits down and switches on and selects a program or website. From the moment the child touches the machine, he or she is in charge. Children have almost unlimited choice of what to do, what to find out and who to contact. They are never made to feel stupid, in the way or unequipped. What

24

they are wearing is unimportant, as is their accent, where they live and how much money they have. The 'relationships' within these programs, or websites, are 'fair' – and any child loves that.

The computer offers choice. In our society there is nothing more important. We expect to have choice in our lives; to choose how we spend our leisure time, where we live, who our neighbours are and where our children go to school. We may only want one item when we shop but we expect plenty of possibilities. On the Internet, as in many of the shops in our towns and cities, the choice seems limitless. To choose gives people a sense of power and control. Children are no exception.

The wondrous Web

Surfing the Net for sites that have been designed to appeal to children is fascinating – and time-consuming. The graphics are imaginative and colourful. The characters are captivating, sometimes sinister, but always strong. The associated merchandise is always promoted on a 'must have' basis. For some examples, search for:

- www.botham.co.uk/kids.htm with lots of fun recipes for young bakers to try.
- www.doodlestudio.com with endless entertainment for a rising artist.
- www.disney.com gives you cartoon fun.
- www.mamamedia.com introduces children to meeting each other – virtually.
- www.neopets.com introduces children to effort-free pets.

- www.bigideas.com is the home of Veggietales.
- www.ala.org/parentspage/greatsites is an American site that lists good sites for children.
- www.beritsbest.com is another site that gives a list of children's sites.

Even with these 'safe' sites, it wouldn't do any harm to install the slogan 'handle with care' as a regularly appearing screensaver.

Education and learning

A snapshot of their school sums up a major aspect of children's lives. Our schools aim to provide every child with a good education, a firm basis on which to build the rest of their lives. Unfortunately many children are growing up in the context of high adult unemployment. Some go to school from homes where their carers may be the third or fourth generation to be unemployed. Increasingly, as they themselves grow up through school, they are filled with questions about what real choice they have.

For many children, the most influential part of their education happens in the streets around their homes. Their learning is tough and starts young. By the time they are 'tweenagers' their low aspirations and expectations may already be well established.

But for the majority of children, school is an exciting and fascinating place. It provides dependable relationships with safe adults and access to new skills and information. It offers the daily opportunity to compete and succeed. For this generation, education opens a door of exploration. Children are encouraged to take responsibility for their education and to revel in their continual achievements.

Protected or at risk?

Children have never been so protected as in our day. Gone are the times when they found their own way to school. Many parents now walk or drive their children to school themselves. The risk of bullying in schools, or on the streets, is high. City services run widespread campaigns to encourage children not to accept bullying.

The 'Don't talk to strangers' campaign of several years ago is still appropriate, but 'not talking' has proved to be inadequate. Children are seen to be in need of physical protection by someone physically bigger than themselves. Finding out where children are going, who will be there, what they will do and when they need to be collected is the perpetual headache of a modern-day parent. So the strange truth is that at a time when children are more streetwise than ever before, they need a caring adult as never before.

Family – friend or foe?

Shockingly, during this time, the family itself has surfaced as being a potentially dangerous place. Child abuse has been exposed in the middle of families or family friendships. Whether there are more examples of it, or it's simply that we know more about it, is hard to say. What we do know is ugly and frightening. Every time a new story is exposed, we wonder how such a situation could continue for so long and still remain a secret. Whether in a family, or within the special provision for children in need, it seems that the people responsible for keeping children safe may be the very ones who pose the greatest risk.

On a less sinister front, family life continues to be a struggle. Many children belong to two homes and divide their lives between them. Some parents are caring for a family as the only adult in the home and juggling their own paid employment with that. What was once the norm for children – a stabilising daily routine at home – is now hard to achieve.

Even with two parents, often both working, family life takes some holding together. Relationships need time to grow. As babies turn into toddlers and then become children, as tweenagers appear and turn subtly into teenagers before our eyes, it is hard to find quality time to nurture them to develop their sense of self-worth and self-confidence. But without it, how can parents ensure that their children are developing as people with whom they will enjoy mutual respect, fun and communication – for the rest of their lives?

These issues are common to all people, regardless of income or education. Leo Tolstoy commented: 'All happy families resemble one another, each unhappy family is unhappy in its own way' (*Anna Karenina*).

The challenge

Out of all these general reflections on childhood today, what are the particular aspects that have implications for Christians?

Parents and teachers

Our society has left adults, at home and at school, in an unenviable position. In both cases, they seem to have been left with responsibility but little authority. They are seen as the key people in the scenario, but little is done to support them or help them to make sense of what is happening.

If they do well, everyone thinks it is no more than they should do. If the children in their care seem to fail, everyone blames the parent or the teacher. Without a sense of their own authority, discipline has become a huge issue for many parents and for most teachers, many of whom live with high levels of fear and stress.

In both contexts, relationship is of the essence. Anne Davis writes:

> Young children will always respond more positively to discipline imposed by adults they love and want to please, and will try harder to gain their approval and praise. Attempts by people they do not know or trust or like to enforce any aspect of discipline will probably be met with resentment, tears or confusion, and are best avoided. As children get older, they will come under the discipline of their teachers. But if the basic groundwork of respect and obedience has not been established in the pre-school years there is little that any teacher can do to make up that deficit – unless with the full, if belated, co-operation of the parents.[5]

Relationships matter. The whole of our lives, as Christian individuals and as local church communities, should show

---

[5] *Confident Parenting* (Souvenir Press, 1997).

that we place our priorities on people rather than on programmes and projects. This concern will show in the way we address people, in the way we welcome newcomers, in how we refuse to make assumptions about people based on age, race, social status or whatever.

Our playgroups and other children's activities should set an example of care and respect. Leaders, parents and children will feel secure because high standards of 'relating' are set and maintained. Wouldn't it be terrific to know that for a harassed young mother, a visit to a church toddlers' group would guarantee much-needed support – and a subtle object lesson in Christlike caring?

What can we do?

The suggestions below are for the reader to follow through or propose to church leaders.

- Encourage parenting skills by running courses where issues can be discussed between groups of parents. Ask parents of older children to pass on what they have learned to those with toddlers and pre-schoolers. Give support to group members as they try out their new skills. Make time for feedback sessions so that people can encourage one another.
- Set up support groups for teachers in local schools. Show teachers your concern is for them and their work, not solely for the children or the reputation of the school. Campaign for the teachers in your local schools to have regular access to a professional counsellor or listener.

- Become involved in community provision for families. Many parents in some areas have had no experience of good parenting themselves. Some are unable to play with their children in a fun or helpful way. Basic support from the community will make an enormous difference to them and to their children – and consequently to local schools.
- Choose to set a challenging pattern for relationships. It is easy to go with the flow and to fall in with modern attitudes. But the local church can make a significant difference in a community by setting an example of alternative lifestyles, for example in terms of loyalty and faithfulness in marriage, commitment and kind humour in friendships, compassion rather than ridicule in relating to children.

Entertainment

Children deserve the best. Everything they receive will not only affect their own minds, attitudes and relationships but also those of the generation to which they will later give birth. Whether we are looking at television or videos, books, theatre or magazines we want to ask for and expect high quality. We need to ensure that entertainment, which has such power to affect young minds, is excellent and worth remembering.

TV and films provide models for relationship-building. Children learn so much through what is presented to them as 'normal'. Unfortunately, some of these very foundational relationships are not handled well by movies and TV soaps and dramas. It is worth making time to view alongside children so that you can discuss the various relationships you see presented.

The problems posed for parents by television used to seem insurmountable. That was before the arrival of the Internet. Now, finding a 'nanny' program to filter the Net has overtaken this challenge of 'What programmes should I let them watch?'

Magazines also have a powerful influence. Many label themselves for one age group while also including an age group several years younger in their target audience. Many girls' magazines, apparently for sixteen-year-olds, give blatant and overt sexual advice to their audience that will include many ten-year-olds. Perhaps this is one of the reasons why sexual initiation comes so early for many children.

Video games and Playstations are an important prerequisite for many of our children. In many games the fantasy element is vitally important. What began twenty years ago with *Dungeons and Dragons* is now a whole generation more sophisticated and enticing. The structure of many games, with the inexhaustible layered approach where each new score introduces the player to another area of the game, means that a new game is seldom short-lived in its attraction. Instead, it offers a solitary challenge and can easily have an addictive quality.

What can we do?

• Take every opportunity to make your voice heard about television and entertainment. Remember that if a programme is on television it is there because people want it. If you disagree with it being shown, make your voice heard. If you have enjoyed something wholesome, make those comments heard too. For comments on BBC output, use www.bbc.co.uk/talk. Contact the Independent Television Commission via www.itc.org.uk. Make contact with the Advertising Standards Authority via www.asa.org.uk.

- Ensure that a Christian voice is heard in local politics to influence issues relating to children.
- Speak to your local MP on points where the law has made bad decisions. 'The law is an ass' is an old slogan, but sadly not out-dated. Make it clear when the law has been the reason for hardship or loss in your area. Find contact details via www.parliament.uk
- Buy a children's or teenagers' magazine simply to get a feel for the attitudes and values it is promoting.

Money

We have never had a more affluent generation of children. Whether the money is in their own pockets or those of their parents, whether their parents are together or apart, many of our children have access to financial resources undreamed of by previous generations. For many children, deprivation is not due to lack of money, but to priorities set for that money by their parents.

At the same time, debt is a problem for many parents. They long to escape from the circle of debt, and yearn to see their children able to handle money wisely. But without access to help and advice, their ambition to live within their means will remain unfulfilled.

What can we do?

- If appropriate to your community, introduce good saving patterns through an organisation such as the Credit Union. Through such a group, people who have never experienced any ability to save and plan take new control over their money. Contact the Association of British Credit Union Ltd at www.abcul.org
- Encourage parents to teach these new-found skills to their children.
- Suggest that the local schools promote the Credit Union scheme.

And finally ...

'What a wonderful world'? Yes, it is – and today's children have a unique opportunity to appreciate how wonderful it is. They have time, energy, imagination, a sense of fun, a sense of amazement and the ability to trust in relationships. In so many ways they are perfectly equipped to enjoy life.

They also have an enormous capacity to appreciate God, to trust him and to enjoy a relationship with him.

In the next chapter we will begin to look at the challenge each local Christian church faces in order to introduce children, in the context of childhood today, to a living faith in Jesus.

Talk about it . . .

- What are some safe ways to become more familiar with a child's culture?
- In what ways does your church support families?
- How does your church support local schools?
- Suggest some ways in which your church can make its voice heard in local politics.
- Can you identify something positive that you have achieved for children near you?

 You can continue this discussion by visiting the web on www.chancetochoose.com

Useful contacts

The Child Poverty Action Group (CPAG)
94 White Lion Street
London N1 9PF
Tel: 020 7837 7979
www.cpag.org.uk

Viva Network
PO Box 633
Oxford OX2 0XZ
Tel: 01865 320100
www.viva.org
Viva Network is an international family of networks set up to link Christians working with 'children at risk' worldwide.

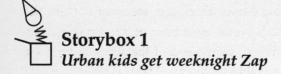

Storybox 1
Urban kids get weeknight Zap

Children and adults can mix in church! St George's Newtown, Birmingham, has proved it. St George's is a small inner-city church in an 'urban priority area'. Its weeknight Zap Club has been a means of outreach and spiritual growth for children – and adults. Judy Johnson, whose husband Robert is Priest-in-Charge, describes how.

Zap Club aims to provide a friendly atmosphere with games, quizzes and teaching songs. We want to allow the love of God to reach through. It's important that the children don't feel they are being preached at. We want to allow God to work through us in all aspects of Zap Club.

It began after we took four children regularly to a similar club in our neighbouring church. The number of children grew to eight, and we realised we should start one on our own premises. We hoped this would encourage other local children to come and join us.

We already had a small group of children meeting during the Sunday morning service. We struggled to find leaders from our tiny congregation. Then a teenager said she would like to lead the Sunday group. One of the leaders met with her once a month to prepare and pray. Then she led the group of children, with another adult keeping her company.

As more people heard about the weeknight club, the numbers increased. Adult members of the congregation wanted to be involved. By the end of the summer term we had about fifteen children coming. Many already came to church. Others started to come because of invitations from their school friends or neighbours. Some of them started coming on Sunday mornings too. Many of them had no other church connections and several came from broken homes.

Following up a personal contact with a church in a wealthy area of the city, we found that their young people wanted to be involved with a children's club in an inner-city area. Our Zap Club sounded ideal. We met to discuss the feasibility, and found out that several young people were interested in joining us on a rota basis.

Plans were set up and these small teams of young people began coming every two weeks. They provided their own programmes, both for games and spiritual activities. Being mainly teenagers, their approach was different, but because our church members were leading the club on alternate weeks we did not lose our own identity.

The young people even had sponsored events to raise money, which they then shared with us. This enabled us to buy items for the club that we could not otherwise afford.

We have also had several evenings for people of all ages. These have included 'It's a knockout' and table games around our hall. The most memorable event was the 'Big Breakfast' two days before Christmas. We cooked and shared a full English breakfast early on Saturday morning and sang carols around the Christmas tree. It was a rare treat so close to Christmas.

When we closed Zap Club for the summer the following year, we had twenty-one names on the register. Not all come every week, but they do keep coming back. We feel excited at how God is using in their lives what goes on both in Zap Club and on Sunday morning.

Our latest venture was to take them in a minibus to a park about thirty minutes' drive away. For some it was their first trip out of Newtown! It was exciting to see them enjoying ball games on the grass, playing on the adventure play-ground and pointing out all the wildlife. The highlight was when my husband went to buy ice creams from the local superstore. Ice creams from a superstore come in bulk, so of course they all had to be eaten. We all did quite well! We found that you don't have to spend lots of money to give simple pleasure to inner-city children.

We have also started to have one service a month for people of all ages. It is very simple and lasts for less than an hour. The children are involved in the service in various ways.

One Sunday, when the service was about the feeding of the five thousand, the children did a survey beforehand about what people liked to eat and drink when they went on a picnic. After the service we took a minibus and two cars to a local tourist spot for a real picnic.

We want to make sure that the various aspects of the life of St George's all fit together. It is a small congregation, but children and adults can enjoy God's life together.

2. 'Picture-Book' People – and More!

What children need to come to faith

Artist David Hockney 'paints' using a camera. He scans a landscape through the viewfinder, clicking as he does so. Later he places the many small views he has exposed to make an overlapping, mosaic 'impression' of the whole landscape. There's no denying that this is an unconventional form of photography, but the resulting images are nevertheless arresting and provocative.

This book may have a Hockney-like quality. Chapter 1 offered snapshots of the world of today's children. Later in Chapter 10, 'What's Been Going On?', focuses on the church and its key developments, research work and innovations that have been significant for work with and for children over the last fifteen years or so.

You may wish to skip forward and scan through the snapshots in that chapter now. It's packed with information that will help put what follows in context. The aim is to address the key question: 'How can we bring together two such divergent groups as today's children and today's church so that children hear the gospel of Jesus and are given a chance to choose?'

What do children need in order to come to faith?

As with anybody else of any age, children need the church to provide three specific things in order for them to have the chance to make a reasonable choice about faith.

They need the facts of faith

They need accurate information about Christianity. This means they need to know what God has said and done through history. Primarily this is Bible knowledge – the sort of information that used to be given in school assemblies and in Scripture lessons.

Past generations received this kind of knowledge in what used to be called 'Sunday school' and often in their homes. This does not mean that it was always well presented – far from it! But the information was available. It was common, not specialist, knowledge. Of course, at that time, ours saw itself as a Christian society and so a lot of this information could be absorbed as well as directly taught.

Even though such information may have been poorly communicated and imperfectly understood, it was truly part of the texture of life. It no longer is, and its absence is significant.

They need 'picture-book' people

If the teacher sharing the facts of faith is a believer, children respond in a totally different way from how they respond when the facts are simply given as information. The believing voice makes a difference. The way in which the events are recounted, the terminology used, the engagement the speaker has with the story – all of these have a totally different impact on the listener, whatever their age.

When a Christian retells what God has said in the past it is as if he or she is also unconsciously saying, 'This is the same God who has spoken into my life.' Or, as they recount what God has done in history, they are unconsciously saying, 'God has worked in my life too.'

The fact is that whatever the words used, a believing speaker has a different impact from one who is cynical or ambivalent about faith. From babyhood, children know when adults mean what they are saying, and the voice of faith is no exception.

This is even more the case when there is opportunity for real relationship to grow between the teacher and the child. It is when real relationships grow – at home, in church or school – that the child sees faith lived out in practice.

Again and again people have spoken about the impact of such a living demonstration of faith in the life of a believer. It's as though God makes us into 'picture-book' people. Our mouths can speak out the facts of faith just as the words in a picture book can be read out loud to tell the story. As children listen to the story, their eyes are looking at the picture.

41

If the pictures do not back up and illustrate the story, children will soon lose interest – the book must have been put together wrongly!

God's 'picture-book' people have a story to tell: their lives are the pictures that illustrate the text of that story. It's the life of Christ lived out through us that convinces our listeners of the validity of what we have to say. Conversely, it is so often our lives that negate that truth – the 'life picture' does not match the story we are telling. For children today to have a chance to choose Jesus, they need to hear accurate information from people whose lives are 'living pictures' of those facts.

Now, the term used here has been 'teacher' rather than 'adult' or 'leader' because the person concerned may be another child or a teenager. This role of handing on the faith is often conveyed through the mouths of friends and family. The important issue, though, is that the responsibility for this has been given to adults. Reading through Deuteronomy 11 gives clear examples: 'Teach them to your children, talking about them when you sit at home and when you walk along the road, when you lie down and when you get up' (Deuteronomy 11:19).

Children undoubtedly can teach, but usually they do so unconsciously. Adults, on the other hand, have a God-given role that includes issues of responsibility and obedience. If the teaching is not being done, then adults should be concerned. Why are they not doing it? Why are they not modelling the teaching role both to children and to other adults? Why are children outside the church not hearing the facts of faith from believing teachers whose lives illustrate the information?

They need to belong before they believe

So, anyone being given the chance to choose the Christian faith needs information from a 'picture-book' person. But they also need to see this teaching lived out in a community of faith, and they need to see this from the inside of the community. In other words, they need a place where they can belong before they believe.

But the belonging must be real! For a person of any age to be willing to come repeatedly into a church community, they need to know that it is a valid place for them to be; one that's right for people like them.

The pattern of belonging and believing can go something like this:

- *Befriending*. A person is befriended, genuinely, because someone in the faith community likes them and wants to enjoy their company.
- *Belonging*. In the context of this friendship, they are invited to belong to their friend's community of faith. They hear the community's facts of faith. They see how these facts are illustrated in their friend's life. They also see how the community is built on the foundation of these facts.
- *Believing*. As the newcomer enjoys this community of faith in the company of people who enjoy doing things that they enjoy, they come to believe what the community believes.

- *Behaving*. As the new believer grows in these beliefs, the way he or she lives changes. Some of these changes are fundamental and noticeable. Some are subtle and happen over a period of time.

Obviously this pattern depends on the work of God in individual lives. So why wasn't God mentioned in the description above? It's because God is at work in all of it. God has been at work in the lives of such people since they began. God is using everything as a way of gaining their attention and drawing them to himself. God loves them!

God uses our friendships, our communities and the Bible to bring people into relationship with himself and to bring change into their lives through the work of his Holy Spirit. It is all God's work. All of us need to notice how God works so that we are open and available for him to use.

Look back at the list of bullet points. What happens after 'Behaving'? What's next for an adult who has joined the community and come to a place of faith and 'life-change'? Well, often they are given a role in the community. They may have had one before of course – it is, after all, one of the ways to confirm that we belong. But often when adults take an overt step of faith and join a church, they quickly find themselves with a role to fill. They have gifts to contribute and part of the pleasure of belonging is to do things together. So they serve the community to which they belong as part of a team whose desire is to honour God in the community and to bring more people to know God through Jesus.

What happens next if it is a child who has joined the community and come to faith? They also need to be given appropriate responsibilities to reflect their growing faith and relationship with the community of faith. For the child, as for the adult, this is the beginning of a path that leads into the whole of the rest of their lives. How they are treated at this stage will influence how they feel about their faith in the future, and it will also act as a model for how they will treat those who are new in the community after them.

In this context the work of Christian summer camps and similar residential holidays is vitally important. While on a camp children hear the facts of faith communicated in a way that perfectly suits their culture. The leaders will have prepared the material properly, will communicate it in innovative ways and will be supported by other team members. The leaders and teachers are living alongside the children for a week or ten days, and become intimately at ease with each other. Friendships made on summer camps often last a lifetime.

All of this happens in the context of a community of faith. Of course it's not a local church, but it is a lively example of faith worked out in community context. Vital work!

Isn't it surprising, then, that so many churches never send their own children on these holidays? So few churches budget in order actively to encourage families to send their children to camp. More ridiculous still is the amazing effort needed each year by CPAS Ventures and Falcon Camps, Crusaders, Scripture Union, Campaigners and other providers of camps and holidays to collect enough leaders to run all their activities. This is vitally important work in evangelism, and the church sleeps on!

What's the problem?

The next challenge is to look at the ideal scenario pictured above and the usual scenario of what happens in our local churches, and to make an honest comparison.

The fact is that children who move from being befriended to the stage of belonging often have no idea that they belong to the church. They may see themselves as belonging to Brownies or to a games club, but they may never realise that they belong to the community belonging to God, where Jesus is the central figure. So, though they might enjoy the club to which their friend has taken them, they never hear the gospel of Jesus explained there. Often, even if the adult leader of the group is a believer, she or he may lack confidence in taking the role of the teacher. Then, because the leader has never modelled that role to the group members, the children who are believers have never learned to be teachers either. In this way the befriending and belonging never lead on to life-changing belief.

Many people are leading a group of children because they feel that if they don't no one else will. They lack any sense of being called by God, valued by the overall church leaders, or equipped in practical terms to do the job well. Many of them came into the role for the wrong reasons: their own children needed a club; they offered to do it temporarily until someone else was found; they did it

Years of 'spiritual starvation' can leave their mark.

because it made them feel they belonged to the community of faith.

Years later some of them still have the same reasons. Their churches have not taken responsibility for teaching them so that they can teach others. Often they fill this leadership role during the only church service in the week, thus missing the only spiritual input available in order to teach children from their own limited knowledge. Even where their own faith was once vibrant, years of 'spiritual starvation' can leave their mark and there is little left for them to give.

47

The training effect

Training makes an enormous difference to such leaders, even if it's only a small amount. During a stimulating training session they begin to believe again. They catch a spark of faith that helps them to believe that children can come to believe. They remember how they used to enjoy the Bible and worship.

Most of all they come to realise that God has called them to hand on their faith to children and that they can only do so if their faith is strong and knowledgeable, leading to teaching that is accurate and lives that are pictures illustrating the facts of faith. They wonder how they have managed to exist through years of leading children's groups without regular training. They realise that they are at risk if they don't regularly receive from the worship and teaching in their own churches.

Of course the trouble is that our churches, regardless of denominational label, do not have a training culture. We expect to get everything free. Training usually costs money and few local churches have a training budget. So when someone is approached to become a children's leader (even when the emphasis is on nurturing the children already within the church community), there is nothing in the mutual agreement about training. The volunteer does not agree to set aside time for training and the church does not agree to pay for it. Usually there is no formal contract between the community and the individual. An individual simply agrees to become a children's leader. It is only as time goes by that they find out what is involved and the church finds out whether they have chosen a good leader or not.

When most churches plan evangelism among children, they look for a team from among the leaders of the existing children's groups. Let's think of it from the leader's point of view. He or she will have had no training or support over possibly years of leadership. Suddenly he or she is expected to respond positively to the suggestion that their role be extended to children from outside the church – children who will not have parents sitting in the congregation and who may not behave in the way churches expect.

Why should such leaders want more children to come into their group at all? After all, they probably already feel trapped in a demanding responsibility at the edge of the church's life.

Sharing resources

Is all this inevitable for every situation? No, definitely not! What could make a difference? Well, for a start, how about some basic organisational training for ministers and other senior church leaders? Such men and women are managers of complex organisations including, as we have seen, large numbers of volunteers. Few of them have had the benefit of training in good management practice. Also we need to acknowledge that not every one of them is a 'people person'. Personality tests show that many ministers and clergy do not come from this category, which means that interacting with people drains them of energy.

Of course, there is nothing to stop such leaders from calling on those in their congregations who have professional training in management and organisation, but from experience it seems that very few leaders do this.

It is also true that members who have such skills tend to be found in the large churches (of whatever denomination) that have a big 'pool' of human resources from which to draw. Their employment leaves them little energy for the demands of active membership in a small struggling church community. In fact, it's unlikely that they will have spare energy to contribute to the big, lively church where they are in membership.

Churches that have such gifted people must be prepared to release them to share their skills with others. We need a fair distribution of the gifts God has given to his church. Of course this will depend on the availability, energy and willingness of those concerned. We need to do more with our existing resources.

If only we stopped ourselves from thinking of evangelism as a sort of inter-church competition, we might free up people who have become stuck in the big, successful, city or suburban churches to be of use further afield. Commissioned in this way, they would still have a secure home base and close friends and supporters who care and pray for them. Thanks to their training in other churches, leaders would be encouraged and enthused. God's treasures would be in wider use. And children, along with many other people, would hear the good news.

Recruiting and training volunteers

Pray for the people you need

God can count. God knows the people you need both to lead the children you already have and to reach out to the children who currently have no chance to choose. The concerned heart of the believer turns to prayer, and when groups of Christians pray together, God loves to work.

Sometimes God's answers to those prayers are amazing – subject matter for bestsellers. Sometimes they are so subtle that it is only in retrospect that people realise what the answer was. If a church has a heart for reaching out to children with the good news of Jesus, you will hear it in their times of prayer together.

Choose the people you need

When looking for leaders for children, it is tempting to assume you should be looking for people who are 'second best'. After all, your best people will already have been chosen to lead adult small groups, to help in worship groups – in fact to lead anything to do with adults.

Please don't go along with that attitude. Challenge it. Children need the best people. They need those who are good at relationships, who can teach the gospel of Jesus clearly, who can answer difficult questions and live the illustrative life of faith. They need the best!

Train the people you need

They may never have led a children's group before. They may have explained the gospel thousands of times to adults and never learned to explain it to children. They may be accustomed to church children who sit still, but how will they cope when their audience gets up or heckles them? They may have come to faith in Christ twenty years ago and have no idea of how children think and behave today. They deserve training and the children they are going to reach deserve them to be trained too.

Grow the people you train

A simple training event or even a series of training events will not produce a team of people ready to launch out to evangelise the children in your neighbourhood. They need to 'grow into' the job, starting with something that is not simply within their ability but within their confidence. You may well find out that someone can swim by throwing them into the deep end of a cold pool, but what will be their attitude to swimming from then on? How much better if, as well as proving they can swim, you grow their pleasure in swimming too!

If you help your leaders to grow from one role to the next, ensuring that you are using their gifts and not over-stretching their confidence, you will find you have a team of confident leaders who love to lead in children's evangelism. Neglect the growing aspect and you may well end up with leaders who let you down and who want to be replaced.

Teach the leaders you grow

The people who end up accepting leadership roles in evangelism with children are not solely children's evangelists. They are also children of God. Like everyone else, they need nurture, support and teaching. Of course, our ministers, pastors and clergy also need to continue to learn, but unlike volunteers they can spend time on this in their own work time. Volunteers serve the church in their 'free' time. Make sure that time for teaching that will grow and stimulate their faith is built into the time they give to the church.

Support the leaders you teach

The idea of delegation has caught on in the church, but in a very misguided way. Here's how it can go. Someone agrees to take on a responsibility in the church. But as soon as they are embroiled in the task, they receive no support, no encouragement, no guidelines for accountability. The buck stops with them because the responsibility has been 'delegated' to them. In fact, this isn't a matter of delegation – this is a description of abdication of responsibility. This can mean that many children's leaders are only answerable to themselves. They have no one to go to if they find the ministry difficult or unrewarding, or if they receive criticism.

Support must be an integral part of the volunteer's ministry with children. They should know who will provide prayer support and who will act as a sounding board for ideas. They should know to whom they will be accountable and to whom they should turn if they receive criticism. All of this should be discussed at the outset between the volunteer and the person responsible for co-ordinating children's work. And it should be set out clearly in a written agreement between church and volunteer.

Encourage the leaders you support

Everybody in ministry needs to be encouraged – not with an empty 'well done' and a pat on the back, but in a proper conversation where performance is talked through in detail. This will provide an opportunity for a senior leader to give feedback on specific matters and to encourage the volunteer by pointing out what they have done well and exploring one aspect that may need some attention.

Be straight with leaders. When you approach new volunteers, be honest with them about what the work will entail. For example, 'You are committing yourself to work every Sunday for a year, apart from the Sundays when there is an all-age service. There will be four training events during the year, which you will be expected to attend. These are the dates . . .' Explain that you will be approaching them towards the end of the year to see if they want to continue on the team. Be clear about times of preparation meetings and meetings for feedback and appraisal.

Be prepared to let them go

Some people persist in ministry with children simply because they fear they would be made to feel ashamed if they gave up. This is not fair on them or on the children they serve. They may well be in the wrong role. If we keep them trapped in this role, they will never want to serve in any other area of the life of the church. It is God who calls us to serve his people in the church and those who are not yet in the church. If someone leaves the team it is God's responsibility to call someone else. So we come full circle back to praying for leaders, whether for evangelism or nurture.

Pray for existing leaders

Pray for the leaders you already have. This is all part of continuing to support them once they agree to take on the role you have suggested. Until then, you may have been praying for them to say 'yes', but once they have accepted, they need your prayers to do a good job and to keep going when it gets tough. They need your prayers that they will be those 'picture-book' people, illustrating truths they teach week by week.

A different approach

When you talk about children's evangelism, do you find that nobody wants to listen? Perhaps it is because people are exhausted and disillusioned by what they are already doing with the children they already have. Perhaps it is time for a different approach.

The suggestions above are for recruiting, training and supporting children's workers. But they are applicable to any network of volunteers in the church, regardless of role or responsibility: children or adults, nurture or evangelism.

These simple steps for growing and keeping a team of highly motivated volunteers offer a solution to the sad situation of never having enough leaders for children in the church.

And finally . . .

If we are going to give children a chance to choose Jesus, we need leaders who are highly motivated and well supported. We need people whose gifts have been recognised and who are involved in this ministry because they know that God has called them and therefore will resource them. We need leaders who have been set apart by the church for evangelism with children. Such leaders are banking on the fact that the church will be committed to training them, supporting them and praying for them.

 Talk about it . . .

- How can we encourage positive attitudes towards training for busy church leaders?
- What insights can we gain from secular organisations as we work with teams of volunteers?
- What are the budget implications of providing good quality training?
- How can a church with limited resources access good training?
- What can we do to ensure a fair share of resources (people, buildings, skills, finances) across the churches?

 You can continue this discussion by visiting the web on www.chancetochoose.com

Storybox 2
Tots build bridges in suburbia

We need to build bridges to help people unfamiliar with church to take that big step over the threshold. Tots Praise at St Mary's Reigate in suburban Surrey has done just that. Held on Monday mornings, it is aimed at mums with pre-school children. Assistant Minister Peter Cunliffe and his wife Rosemary describe how it works.

Tots Praise began out of the desire to connect young families on the edge of the church with the congregation that meets on Sunday. By providing an opportunity for pre-school children to be in the church building, we hoped they would own the church as their place from birth. It was also designed to help the members of the church-run toddler group to move from the church hall through the big doors into the 'sacred space'.

A key feature of Tots Praise is that parents can turn up and not have to do anything. We have no rota for parents. Each child is greeted personally when they arrive. They are all registered and receive a hand-drawn fish-symbol sticky label with their name on it.

Then there are drinks for everyone and hula-hoops for the children, served by retired people from our congregation.

The children collect the potato rings on their fingers, and a drink. This solved the need to provide gluten-free food for two of the children. These have now become a treat associated with Tots Praise. They enjoy these refreshments in the spacious entrance area of the building.

When it's time to start we ring a bell. Then we all walk to the chancel at the opposite end of our twelfth-century church. We sing our own song as we go: 'We're coming to church to praise our God' to the tune of 'Here we go round the mulberry bush'.

John, a retired teacher and lay reader, acts as doorman to ensure that no child leaves without a parent or guardian. He also helps those with buggies through the doorway. Each member of the team plays a crucial role in serving visitors, especially those with more than one child. Many mums have commented on how they appreciate having male role models for their young children.

Once seated in a carpeted area we sing again before telling a Bible story. We use a combination of 'big books', flip charts and drama, encouraging participation and imagination. The curriculum is repeated each year so that children and parents grow familiar with the stories as they hear them again and again.

After the story there is a 'stick and paste' activity on the carpet where they are sitting. This gives them something to take home and share with the rest of the family.

Many dads have found themselves responding to the requests of their children to take a Monday morning off and come to Tots Praise. We long for parents to make connections between Christian truths and the parenting of their children.

The children take a bag around to receive a small collection to help cover costs. Then we celebrate birthdays with an adaptation of 'Happy Birthday', lighting a candle and praying for the birthday child.

Next comes our prayer time. We begin by blowing bubbles, reminding all present that our prayers rise like bubbles and although our words are gone, like the bubbles, our heavenly Father hears and gathers our prayers. We use a chalkboard to collect 'please' and 'thank you' prayers. People contribute to it during the arrival time. Sometimes we have children praying for another family member. Often mums will kneel while the children lay hands on them and pray. Our own faith has grown as we have experienced God answering some big prayers. We also pray for the pre-school children of our mission partners. We use enlarged photographs so that when they come home they are familiar to our children.

After prayers we sing and praise using bells and shakers. We have lots of action songs, some favourites repeated every week. Then comes some quiet as we say Psalm 23 together. This is accompanied by actions. Parents are surprised to find their little ones reciting the psalm to themselves at home. To conclude we sing the grace to one another and give a clap for Jesus.

At the end of the year we give each child a gift. These have included a tape of Christian songs and a Bible storybook to reinforce the message we are giving.

We have come to see that Monday mornings are not simply a step into a church building. Tots Praise offers fellowship, God's word, prayer and worship. This is church itself.

3. Leading Edge
Training future ministers in colleges and courses

The snake of oddly assorted children makes its drunken way across the crowded playground. Those involved in 'let's pretend' or using skipping ropes momentarily stop to watch its gyrations. The game of football simply ploughs through the middle of its line. The child at the front flaps like a bird, trumpets like an elephant or merely dances and skips. With the slight hesitation that produces a Mexican wave, the rest of the line copies her. The season of 'follow my leader' has come round again!

Leadership

'Follow my leader' is not always a game. In some situations it is as serious as life itself. The leadership of any group is vitally important, especially for those working directly under the leader. So much of the content and character of what is done in a community comes from the leader. The leader may be the one at the top of an organisation, or leading from the front of a team. Through their immediate colleagues they influence the whole community. James Dunn comments:

> The leadership issue remains complex . . . it is a special kind of influence which works in situations where results are needed. It touches people and involves them in the process. Often these 'results' do not exactly coincide with personal goals, but they require a spirit of togetherness and a co-ordination of effort if they are to be achieved. This means that as well as a blossoming forth of individuals, there often has to be a bending of wills and sometimes of backs, in the interests of reaching a common goal. True leadership creates and sustains these conditions.[1]

The role of leader, either singly or as part of a group, is a complex one. It can combine so many other roles – those of manager, director, model, mentor, coach, teacher and enabler. Leadership is the key role that ensures that a group makes progress. That progress will be the reason for the existence of that group.

Leadership in the church

The church exists to nurture an increasing number of healthy Christians of every age. That's what it is for. Jesus said, 'Therefore go and make disciples of all nations, baptising

---

[1] James Dunn, *The Effective Leader* (Kingsway, 1995).

them in the name of the Father and of the Son and of the Holy Spirit, and teaching them to obey everything I have commanded you' (Matthew 28:19–20). The effectiveness of the leader of a local church is gauged by what is happening under that leadership: how is the church obeying Jesus' commission?

Of course, not every church leader must be skilled and competent in working with children. But unless all leaders are concerned for this area in the life of their church, unless they are actively encouraging its success and well being, they are not effectively leading that church. The disciples their church makes will be adults; the children growing up around that church will never have the chance to choose Jesus.

Tradition

Many church leaders would not welcome this view of their ministry. Traditionally, the minister has appointed someone to oversee the work with children and the chosen children's worker has simply got on with it, sometimes without any support. Often the main criterion for choosing such a person has been that they are good with children or that they have been a Sunday school teacher all their lives.

The trouble is that once they are appointed they will be leading a team of adults. Such leadership does not demand the same skills as those needed for being a children's leader. The skills are not necessarily transferable. The leader of such a team needs support from a good senior leader/manager.

They need to be directed by the person who is directing the church. The direction set for the church must be reflected in the direction set for its children's work.

Key skills

The minister is leader of the church, and 'church' means children as well as adults, the youth as well as the elderly. The church is for people of all ages. The minister should work with a 'generation to generation' attitude to faith sharing and see this as the fundamental activity to which the church is committed.

If a definition of the minister is that she or he is the leader of leaders, this will affect the gifts and skills needed to do the job. The minister will need to be proficient in management, organisation and communication skills. The lack of these gifts and skills will have an adverse effect on work with children in the church and on evangelism with children outside the church.

Leaders should not easily feel threatened. They need to be people who delight in the successful ministry of someone they are leading. They will see people joining the church community through the doorway of its children's outreach, and they will genuinely rejoice over this. They will have a real appetite for releasing less-experienced people into leadership, and they will have an eye for recognising potential gifts. They will see young or relatively inexperienced leaders flourishing in children's leadership and will be excited by this growing resource in the church.

Leaders should not easily feel threatened.

Church leaders should understand and model accountability. Jesus knew what it was to have authority and to be under authority (Luke 7:1–10). Leaders will be careful to set clear lines of accountability throughout the church. Everyone will have appropriate challenges. It also means that everyone will have encouraging support, including those working with children.

Finally, the overall minister's biblical perspective, especially regarding evangelism, is crucially important. With a strong biblical base, good children's evangelism will be effective and sustained in the life of the church. Regular and reliable Bible teaching for the whole congregation will have a significant effect on every decision that is made.

The training gap

Let us focus now on matters relating to the training given to prospective church leaders in our theological colleges.

When it comes to the provision of training, it is difficult to break with tradition. For example, there's a well-established assumption that the minister does not need to know much about either children or management. Of course, many people come into the ordained ministry from senior secular positions where they have had experience of fulfilling an organisational role. A few others have had their first taste of church leadership by being leaders of children's groups. But many more have had neither of these advantages.

Sadly, it is unlikely that our training colleges will identify such lack of experience as a gap that needs filling. The courses taken by many trainees will be strongly theological and theoretical. Our colleges do not see that their courses should prepare students for all of the practical demands of ministry in the local church. Rather, they view the years of training as a unique opportunity to have quality time for the vital theological study a church leader needs. And of course they are right – it *is* vitally important.

Unfortunately, from the beginning of their time in the local church, new ministers will be expected to be leaders and to operate as managers. From the beginning, whether they feel qualified to do so or not, they will have important roles to play. They will be guiding teams of volunteers and heading up crucial areas of the church's ministry, including children's evangelism.

When prospective candidates are assessed for their suitability for leadership they are usually assessed on a variety of gifts and skills. The list is unlikely to include experience with children or with evangelism. Those who choose these vitally important people are looking for students who can grapple with theological study. They want people who will be able to think through the important issues of their future ministry. Even on more practically based courses, it is rare for someone to be accepted on the basis of their experience with children, unless it is for a specific children's leadership course. It is fair to say that those in charge of selection place a low priority on experience with children.

This is potentially disastrous. As far as the normal courses for theological training of our main denominations are concerned, not one of the colleges I have approached has been able to claim that their theological study will include the young. For example, a course may include a module on pastoral care, but it is unusual to find a component on the pastoral care of children within it. Study of the subject of bereavement might include the issue of caring for adults bereft of a child. It does not usually include the issue of caring for a bereaved child. Even where a course director ensures that the subject of children is introduced at some time during a course, it is likely that the chosen topic will be the nurture of children in the church. The chosen topics are more likely to be Sunday groups, children and communion, or all-age worship.

The problem starts with those who teach such courses. An understanding of the theology of childhood is not considered necessary for belonging to a faculty providing theological education. At best, it is seen as an extra. Perhaps it is considered lightweight compared with the ability to apply good theological thinking to the practice of the adult church. Consequently, there are few tutors able to support and develop this area of theological education in terms of teaching, research and the publication of papers and textbooks.

When a student chooses a child-related assignment and looks at the literary support available on the library shelves, he or she will find very little on the theology of childhood. Any authors who are available are probably known more for their practical expertise than for their theological academic achievement – or are unfamiliar names from the USA who might be viewed with suspicion.

What can we do?

Recent research[2] indicates an accelerating decline in the number of children in the church. How can the church break into this cycle of spiralling disaster

- if colleges are not providing the church with ministers who can think theologically about childhood;
- if evangelism among children has not been identified as a key missing element in church life across the denominations;

---

[2] *The Tide Is Running Out* (Christian Research, 2000).

- if new ministers are not able and prepared to lead others in their thinking and practice with children?

Include children in every appropriate subject

I am convinced that we need an all-age approach to theological study. Whatever the subject, courses should explore the implications for people of any age. Students need the discipline of thinking from the perspective of the old and the young, as well as from that of the general population in between.

Required practical experience

Interviewers of prospective students should ask them about their experience in children's evangelism. There may only be bad experience, or none. If so, there needs to be the encouragement that at some time on the course this lack will be remedied. The student should be required to choose a practical assignment with children from outside the church. This might be in the form of a vacation residential camp or a weekly church placement.

The need for academic books

How do we encourage and commission reliable theological study about childhood? Little such work has been commissioned to date. A theologian will usually write up work that has been the subject of his or her own research and private study, but there is no reason why this needs to remain the process.

If this lack of books has a bearing on the present crisis, why not look at a different process for achieving a more satisfactory end? Maybe those with responsibility for theological study should consider commissioning books that explore the theology of childhood from good, reliable theologians.

Child-friendly tutors

Colleges should employ tutors who are prepared to rethink their material. If courses are presented with an all-age, child-inclusive balance, students will be trained to think in that way too. Perhaps each college could appoint one research fellow who would spend three years studying an aspect of the theology of childhood. At the same time they would affect the thinking and approach of both students and staff. Their conversation in both staff and student groups would have a depth of influence. This would make a considerable difference to the way in which all theological study is approached.

It is true that funding is needed to implement some of these changes. The good news is that concern about children's evangelism is now in the air. We need to explore ways of releasing funds for such projects. Change can be implemented and children with no Christian relatives can be given a chance. It is their rightful inheritance.

The trainees' tales

Here are two true stories based on the experience of contemporary trainees for full-time ministry.

Elizabeth

Elizabeth is an ordinand, accepted for training for the Anglican ministry. Her three years at college are divided into two years of serious academic study, followed by a year on ministerial issues. During her first few weeks at college, she is introduced to the local church where she will be a visiting student for the whole of her first term. She visits the minister and meets his staff. She is assigned to a home group. As the term goes by she gets to know this group of adults. They are warm-hearted and welcoming, inviting her for meals and other social events. She takes an increasing role in leading Sunday services and is sometimes asked to contribute to the midweek prayer and worship evening.

As her college work continues, Elizabeth is encouraged and taught to think theologically on a wide range of subjects. Her mind always turns to her placement church for her illustrations, and to her former work in the legal profession. Before college her main experience of ministry involved helping to lead a home group and assisting with visiting. When she spends time in the college library with a list of ministerial essay titles in her hand, she finds a good selection of books that help her explore the subjects that most appeal to her. She tends to choose those connected to her own knowledge and experience.

Elizabeth is stimulated by the study of the Bible. She finds that she is almost completely unfamiliar with some of the books she discovers. Her tutors are good teachers and their expertise thrills her. She delights in the whole process of reading, essay preparation and tutorials exploring a wide variety of topics.

As the course continues, new local-church placements help to broaden her experience of pastoral care. She joins other members of staff on funeral and hospital visits. In her final year, she is faced with choices about practical courses. She decides to deepen her knowledge of the issues where she has felt most inexperienced. She chooses a counselling course on caring for the dying run by a hospice chaplain, and another on creative teaching methods. She is able to try out some of what she is learning with the home group in her placement church.

Finally, Elizabeth visits a church in the area in which she will serve at the end of her training. She spends time with the minister and other staff talking about what she has experienced in college and finding out about the kind of ministry going on in that parish. They get to know each other and decide that a good working relationship could be achieved. They begin to make links between the needs of the parish and the gifts and skills that Elizabeth is bringing with her. For the first time, someone mentions the need for her to manage the church's rota of struggling children's leaders. They hope Elizabeth will be able to develop a strategy for growth in the church's children's work.

Elizabeth reviews the previous five years of her life. She is unable to identify anything that will resource her for this challenge.

Paul

Paul has been accepted for training at an independent Bible college. He was a teacher, and has spent several years working as a part-time youth worker in his home church, often taking young people away on camps and getting involved in local schools.

People trust Paul because he is good at what he does. He has worked on his own a lot, where he was being paid to do the work, so people left it to him – an arrangement he liked anyway.

He is young and energetic, popular with the other students. They find him an excellent resource when they need help preparing a school assembly or a talk for a youth group on their church placements.

Paul finds some of his course work frustrating. The emphasis on theology is fairly stimulating but he always wants to get on to the practical implications long before the tutor does. Similarly, in seminar groups Paul finds it hard to hide his impatience when people discuss a theological point for the whole of the session. He wants to say that church life is not like this; that it's about people who want to *do* things, not talk about them. Paul argues that if the church doesn't get its act together it will lose all its young people.

Paul always finds himself thinking 'youth' when others are obviously thinking 'adults'. He feels that God has called him to be a full-time minister in the church. He knows that with his background and experience he may well start off in a large church. There would then be more than one minister and he would be able to maintain his interest and expertise with young people. He expects churches will jump at the opportunity to have him on their leadership team.

One of Paul's tutors is involved in a local children's initiative. The tutor leads an extra-curricular day on evangelism with children. Paul chooses not to go. He feels that younger children are not 'his thing'. Anyway, to Paul evangelism with children sounds confusing. He considers them too young to make decisions about their lives. Paul's only experience of church-based children's work is the one occasion when, as a boy, he went to Sunday school with a friend. Occasionally he has seen children's groups operating at his own church, through an open door. It all looked fairly static and boring – not something he wanted to know more about. Children's work was probably something best left to women or those who had children of their own.

Paul's hopes for his future are fulfilled. A church that is local to the college approaches him. They invite him to visit and to see if he will 'fit'. He is stimulated by what he discovers. The services contain good presentations using modern projectors. The youth work is great. A large group of members congregate after the evening service to meet him. The young people seem to have an excellent relationship with the good team of people leading them. Paul takes the job.

The early days of Paul's time in the church feel strange. The youth work is organised and energetic. It's in such good order that Paul feels a bit sidelined. He looks forward to meeting with the youth leaders' team once a month for planning and prayer, but he is slightly disconcerted to find that he is expected to do the same with the team of children's leaders. He is not sure what to do at either evening.

At a particular youth leaders' meeting, there's discussion about a situation that has arisen in the church. There is a conflict between the offspring of two church families, and now the parents are also involved. The leaders disagree over the right way to tackle this situation. Paul openly agrees with one of the opinions offered and suddenly the whole meeting becomes volatile.

Later, as he goes for his meeting with the children's leaders, he resolves to sit back and listen to them. Paul finds that the group is silent as he enters the room. He begins by asking them about themselves and why they are involved with leading children. He asks them how they feel about developing the groups and inviting children in from outside the church. He suggests ideas – alternatives to the Sunday school experience that he had had as a child. The group lapses into silence again.

Paul reviews the two evenings. He looks back over the previous four years of his life for the experience and knowledge that will help him lead two teams of adults. He admits to himself that he knows nothing about children and is not interested in them. He also admits that he would much rather do youth work than lead others doing it. Paul faces the fact that in order to do his job well he needs to know about management and about children's work.

Talk about it ...

- The agreeable stranger you're chatting to at a party turns out to be the principal of a training college. What would you like to say to her/him to ensure that future ministers for your church receive appropriate training in children's evangelism?
- What should a local church do when a new minister arrives with no experience or knowledge of children's evangelism?
- How can we make sure that people offering themselves for training have at least some experience of children?
- What can be done to ensure new, high quality writing on the theology of childhood?
- What can we do to encourage the development of a truly all-age church?

 You can continue this discussion by visiting the web on www.chancetochoose.com

Useful contacts

London Bible College
Green Lane
Northwood HA6 2UW
Principal: The Revd Dr Derek Tidball BA, BD, PhD
www.londonbiblecollege.ac.uk
mailbox@londonbiblecollege.ac.uk

The Queen's College
Somerset Road
Edgbaston
Birmingham B15 2QH
Principal: The Revd Peter Fisher
www.queens.ac.uk
queens.college@compuserve.com

Ridley Hall
Sidgwick Avenue
Cambridge CB3 9HG
Principal: The Revd Dr Christopher Cocksworth
www.ridley.cam.ac.uk
jb215@cam.ac.uk

St John's College
Chilwell Lane
Bramcote
Nottingham NG9 3DS
Principal: Canon Dr Christina Baxter
www.stjohns.nottm.ac.uk
college@stjohns.nottm.ac.uk

Spurgeon's College
189 South Norwood Hill
London SE25 6DJ
Principal: Dr Nigel Wright
www.spurgeons.ac.uk
enquiries@spurgeons.ac.uk

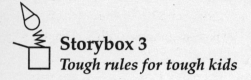

Storybox 3
Tough rules for tough kids

Bishop James Jones of Liverpool has commended Kidz Klub as 'one of the best ways of showing children they have a place in God's kingdom'. We asked Geoff Pearson, Vicar of St Bartholomew's in Roby, Liverpool, to describe the Kidz Klub based at Trinity Church, an ecumenical church in Page Moss. It's an area of high unemployment, crime and drug abuse.

Imagine the scene: the lights dim, the countdown begins. The leaders enter the stage accompanied by bright lights, music, balloons and cheers. The rules are sung:

- Rule number one is stay in your seat.
- Rule number two is obey your team captain.
- Rule number three is the whistle means silence.

It's time for Kidz Klub to start.

Kidz Klub provides a fast-moving mix of games, drama, video, story-telling and worship. The leaders set out to give the children a truly exciting and dynamic hour in their week. The loud magazine-style programme does not exclude times of rich silence.

There is a strong and clear policy of discipline. Leaders prepare so as to ensure a sound grasp of the Bible material. They will also have an understanding of current cartoon characters. They may even have negotiated with McDonald's for suitable prizes.

Kidz Klub happens on Thursday evenings. There are different time slots for the age groups: 4–7s meet 4.00–5.00 pm; 8–11s meet 5.30–6.30 pm and over 11s (called TNT) meet at 7.15 pm.

Each week four core values are brought into the programme:

- God loves me.
- I have sinned.
- Jesus died for me.
- I must now decide to live for God.

There's an opening prayer and four or five fast, loud, action songs. Then we have energetic and exciting games. We celebrate birthdays. We have a special competition open to those who have brought friends for the first time. Then we judge the memory verse sheets that have been coloured in.

Before the teaching time we review the rules. The boys' group and girls' group each has four balloons. Any bad behaviour results in one balloon being popped. If all the boys' balloons are popped during the Klub none of the boys receive any sweets. Worse still, their sweets are given to the girls! The reverse applies.

Each week the teaching time contains a one-concept

lesson taken from the Bible. It includes a memory verse, Bible lesson and several object lessons. These are communicated creatively using puppets, drama, OHP, video or slides. There is also a weekly instalment of a life story that helps the children apply the Bible to real situations.

But it doesn't end there. Visiting is essential. This provides the relational element that is not possible when Kidz Klub meets. Each week we visit over 300 children in their homes. Our reason is to hand out a sheet with the week's memory verse printed on it. We also take any information about the next Kidz Klub.

This is a priority and visitors come to see it as a highlight in their week. Bishop James Jones recently went visiting with two of our team. He asked the children what they liked about Kidz Klub. Replies varied from games, prizes, and leaders dressing up in costume to 'I hear about Jesus and how special I am'.

Two churches within one Anglican parish resource our Kidz Klub. Alongside it we also have a variety of children's ministries including uniformed organisations and more traditional Sunday activities.

We need as much gospel input into young lives as possible. Although we contend that Kidz Klub is an appropriate model of church for children today we know it is often in smaller groups that further 'discipling' takes place.

Evangelist Bill Wilson from Metro Ministries in New York pioneers the resources used by most Kidz Klubs. He runs an enormous Kidz Klub in Brooklyn with up to 20,000 children a week. Before moving to New York over twenty years ago,

Wilson developed a Sunday school curriculum and adopted a strategy of 'Publicise, visit, bring by bus'. He wanted a 'holiday Bible club' atmosphere to be recreated on a weekly basis. Fuelled by belief in the life-and-death issues at stake, Wilson and his team desperately want each child to know that God loves them personally. They want each child to know that at least one person is crazy about them.

So do we. Our vision as a church is to seek to reintroduce Christianity into our society. Kidz Klub is part of that vision as we aim to influence a new generation and change a culture.

4. Keeping Going
Ongoing training of working ministers

'Well, here's the dog collar, this is the key to the manse – and let me introduce you to the caretaker.'

Life for a brand-new minister (or assistant minister) is a steep learning curve. Situations they find themselves in vary according to denomination and geography. In some they will still be seen as trainees under the ongoing guidance of a senior colleague. Or they may join a team of ministers in a cluster of churches. In this situation, fellow team members can act as a protection between them and other people's expectations.

Others will be in a more isolated, exposed situation. They may find that they have the entire responsibility for a congregation. They may find that their only available colleague leads a neighbouring church. In this situation the new minister may find that serving the needs of his or her church is an overwhelming new experience.

Great expectations?

Whatever the situation, the majority of such new ministers are likely to have a brief that includes the care of the young. Traditionally this has been the case and shows little sign of changing. This is understandable. The new minister is usually younger than the senior colleague and frequently arrives out of college with a young family. This would appear to be an excellent qualification for children's work – with the bonus of a built-in support system. Any new minister also appears to have the energising benefit of recent training. Everyone else is weary, so expecting the newcomer to contribute to this major and challenging area of the life of the church seems reasonable.

'The young' is only one of a plethora of issues and groups with which new ministers will need to grapple in their early ministry. They will need to become familiar with the public services provided by their church and with its home-group system. They will need to get to know the members of the governing body of the church, and spend time with the housebound and the elderly. They will need to become familiar with the institutions in the community with which they must build a relationship: hospitals, schools, residential homes, local shops and businesses. It all takes time and energy.

'The young' includes a wide range of challenges too. For many churches this age group is identified as those aged from birth to eighteen. In some it will also include students. The new minister could find he or she has responsibility for (take a deep breath) overseeing the crèche, pram service, toddler group, Sunday children's groups, midweek children's groups, youth group, assemblies in local schools, visits of the local school to the church, training in parenting skills, training leaders of children's and youth groups, planning all-age services, and sorting out the church's child protection policy. In each area, the minister will be expected to make the vital link between the young and the old, the church and the local community, those inside the church and those outside.

Many first-time ministers arrive in their new posts with families that have already experienced the turbulence of two or three years in temporary college accommodation. They arrive knowing that in three or four years' time they will be on the move again. So new ministers not only have to cope with the onslaught of ministry, many aspects of which are completely new; they also have to love and honour their own family members in their upheaval.

New ministers are under pressure to deliver. They are expected to 'hit the ground running'. Having waited for the new minister to arrive, most church members will have high expectations. Some aspects of church life will have been 'on hold' pending the minister's arrival. Others will have been handled on a temporary basis by the senior, overworked colleague, or by a church member. Either way, the arrival of the new person will be a signal for relief and anticipation.

Within this setting, it is easy to see why children's evangelism is unlikely to be top of the new minister's priority list. Probably they have not been encouraged to give much thought to it during their college course. They may have received no training prior to that. Now, under a deluge of new responsibility, it is rare for children's evangelism to feature in their weekly work.

Training for new ministers is usually available, and may be provided by their denomination. There may even be an official expectation that they will attend a certain number of study days. They may be required to develop their competence in certain areas of ministry.

Or the expectation may be that the minister has recently come from a period of study and training. Anything further must be fitted in as and when possible, perhaps via the mentoring of a senior colleague.

In some denominations groups of newly appointed ministers plan their own training in order to ensure that the programme is relevant to them. In most cases topics on offer usually include pastoral care issues such as bereavement and the practicalities of preparing people for baptism, marriage, confirmation and so on. It often includes subjects such as time-management and stress.

Many other church organisations offer training that would help ministers. Some even offer an incentive for children's leaders to bring their minister with them when attending a training day. A major concern is to find ways of enticing ministers to sign up for training on nurture and evangelism with children.

In brief

The church has access to gifted new leaders. They come to their church responsibilities after years of excellent teaching and perhaps considerable practical experience. They oversee the work being done with children by teams of committed volunteers. Ongoing training and ministerial development is available for them. Yet despite this, we are failing to reach children outside the church. And we are losing the ones we already have.

What's the problem?

It goes back to the absence of any requirement for ministers to think theologically about the young. Even when faced with the practical responsibilities of running a local church, there is nothing to jolt a new minister into hunger for this kind of training or teaching. This describes the common context for new ministers. Although the starting point in each denomination is slightly different, there is a disconcerting similarity between them.

The massive demands of the first years of ministry encourage the 'survival mode' habit, which sadly can last a lifetime. It is hard to find time and energy for personal training. In the denominations where regular training is provided, there is often reluctance on the part of the church to release ministers to take it up. The level of attendance demanded is very low and the choice of which days to attend is usually left to the minister. The ministers themselves choose from the subjects on offer. What subjects are they most likely to choose? Those about which they feel most pressurised. They rarely choose a training day on provision for the young. The only subject inclusive of children that appears regularly is that of all-age services.

Many churches have young families in their congregations. In most of them, those who value it most – the young parents – hold provision for young children in place. They always seem well able to provide for the children in their care. The ministers rarely, if ever, listen to what they are teaching the children since they are busy at the time, leading the adult service. The only time a minister is likely to get involved with child provision is when leaders are in short supply. Then the provision becomes a practical challenge rather than an obvious training need.

Ministers will occasionally become involved in children's evangelism, for example with a holiday Bible club. But without the challenge of training and introduction of new thinking, they are likely to use an old formula rather than really engage with the issues.

So, even when training is provided, the topics of children and children's evangelism are unlikely to feature on ministerial training programmes. Evangelism among children will lead to an increase of children in the church. This will cause an increased demand for children's leaders, something that will often involve the minister. This means that training for evangelism with children will not actually solve any ministerial problems. It might expand them.

What if?

What would happen if churches across the denominations provided essential training on

- organisation of volunteer teams;
- planning long-term strategy for ministry;
- evangelism and nurture among children?

If new ministers were actively encouraged to grapple with these issues in their early years, the impact that our churches make on children would be radically different. In my opinion, it would lead to a 'paradigm change'.

Teams of volunteer leaders would be carefully chosen and well trained. Becoming a children's leader would be a positive experience, and such leaders would be supported. They would know how they fitted into the church's strategy for the young, and they would not only feel valued themselves, they would be energised and excited by the 'big picture'.

The whole church would become involved in prayer and special events. There would be regular teaching from an involved and committed minister about children and their place in God's kingdom.

Children outside the church would have a chance. There would be opportunities for them to belong to the church and to hear the gospel. They would experience the presence of God, they would be involved in what was happening as God's people worshipped him and shared their lives together, and they would have the chance to choose Jesus.

The whole church would be strengthened. Children would grow up into the teenage and adult groups, and they would understand about evangelism because they would have grown up with it.

It is so easy for the minister, vicar, pastor or curate to remain unchallenged by the needs of the children inside and outside the church. If they, the leaders, are unconcerned by the needs of the children within the faith community and those unreached by the gospel, why should anyone else be bothered?

Training matters

Provide a basic training scheme

The present situation would change if every church community were able to offer new ministers a basic cluster of subjects for training and experience. It would include evangelism among children, the content having been agreed across the denominations. There should be a recognised qualification for successful completion of these courses that would probably continue for the first four years of ministry.

The aim

Everyone has different abilities. Some have more of a natural affinity with children than others. The aim is not to turn the trainees into children's ministers. Rather it is to equip them to take responsibility for the children's ministry of their church. Their training and study would resource them to manage those accountable to them. It would give them confidence in the questions and concerns that would ensure that this vitally important ministry is being fruitful.

Flexible provision

Training could be provided directly through denominational structures and personnel. Alternatively, it could be selected from the training on offer from national organisations and agencies, or it could be achieved through on-the-job supervision. There should be a balance between practical experience and theological input. Child development should be included.

Training should answer the questions 'What?' and 'Why?', as well as 'How?' Most leaders of children's groups are looking for lots of good ideas. That is what will make the difference to the next meeting of the group. But a stream of ideas for activity on its own is not enough. Activities must be based on right thinking, otherwise they simply entertain. Evangelism aims at more than that.

Content

Learning to delegate. Ministry among children is dependent on volunteer leaders, many of whom are untrained. But the work of reaching children outside the church is too important to be abandoned to leaders who have been left to their own devices. It must have the knowledgeable oversight of caring, concerned and properly supported leaders. In other words, it must be carefully delegated.

Delegation is a skill that can be learned. As training guru Bryn Hughes points out, few people automatically delegate well, but it is simple to train anyone to do so using good principles.[1] There are professional organisations that spe-

---

[1] Bryn Hughes, *Leadership Tool Kit* (Kingsway, 2002).

cialise in team building and getting the best out of team members. Their trainers will deal with delegation too since it is an intrinsic element of a team.

Delegation is a skill that can be learned.

Learning to manage. Ministers are usually aware of their need to manage their own time and resources. They are often less aware of their role as the managers of large numbers of volunteers who should be accountable to them. Many of these are children's leaders.

If ministers are to galvanise these teams into focused and profitable action, basic management must be part of their training, regardless of the level of formality within their team arrangements.

Such training will include:

- selecting leaders, both paid and voluntary;
- agreeing conditions so that everyone knows what is expected;
- ensuring that commitment to training, accountability and review is built into the agreement.

Learning to plan strategically. Ministers need training to ensure that children's work has a strategy, and that such a strategy is part of a 'whole church' plan for mission and evangelism.

Unfortunately the nature of church life is such that unless this forward-planning aspect of ministry is emphasised, it will not happen. Most ministers are rushed off their feet. Too often they make decisions on the basis of the 'tyranny of the urgent over the important'.

With this in mind, training in 'big picture' strategic planning is an essential – something that the local church is right to expect to be provided for its leaders. This training is available in the UK from organisations such as CPAS and Administry.

Studying the theology of childhood. Part of the minister's job is to think through the biblical and theological issues surrounding children and evangelism. Unless they do, it is unlikely that their church members will.

In the UK and Ireland we have plenty of able theologians. Let's invite them to clergy gatherings and ministers' meetings to share their insights and understanding, and to engage in discussion. This would raise the profile of the theology of the child. Children's evangelism would gain respectability. Ministers would be stimulated to think about the young, and there would be an immediate effect on the practice in their churches.

Training for inclusiveness. Ministers should be in touch with what church life means to *all* people, regardless of age group, ability, marital status and so on. The life of the local church can successfully include a variety of experiences and expectations that can be fitted together creatively and functionally.

As individuals we see issues from the point of view of our own experience. When we are young parents, we are concerned about good child provision or innovative all-age services. When we become grandparents, we may suddenly become aware of a renewed interest in young children that may have been absent for years. An unmarried minister will probably be aware of the needs of the single people in the congregation. A minister living with disability will be aware of others who face similar challenges – and so on.

God's aim is that every church community should become a welcoming place for all people. Even if a church has group leadership, it will probably be composed of people who have similar life experience. Church leaders need opportunities to think through cross-age, inclusiveness issues. Training should involve stimulation to imagine provision for the young, the elderly, the single and the unemployed. The minister will never be a member of all those categories, but all ministers lead people who are members of some of them.

Such increased awareness will make a difference to provision for children's evangelism and to the status of evangelism throughout the whole church. Training will give the minister the skill to handle a growing network of relationships.

Going visiting. A leader should resist accepting too readily that the practice in his or her church is the norm. Every church is different. One of the most stimulating and stress-free ways to gain new insights is to visit other churches. It is worth ensuring that the church being visited is in a similar social situation to that of the visitor, and it is helpful if it is not too local.

But how could such visits be arranged? How about a website dedicated to children's evangelism, on which church leaders could contact one another and arrange meetings and visits? The website would provide a forum for swapping information as well as arranging visits. Leaders could contact colleagues whose churches are already involved with the kind of children's evangelism they may be considering. Visits could be a great source of mutual encouragement, with people learning from one another's insights, successes and mistakes, and supporting one another through the early stages of new initiatives. Such encouragement could make all the difference between new work being sustained or stopping because of initial difficulties.

Sharing in training

If possible, ministers should accompany their children's leaders on training courses. They are not going to end up on the children's team themselves, but they need to understand the issues that affect their volunteers.

Most organisations that offer this kind of training provide it from central events to which many churches are invited to send delegates. Some trainers will visit a local church in order to provide tailor-made input for that church's team of volunteers. They may suggest that other local churches join in, as they are likely to be ministering in a similar situation. Contacts made at such events can be a good source of ongoing mutual encouragement.

When ministers attend such events they become involved in the discussions, and may be challenged. They could learn answers – and they will be doing all this with their ministerial colleagues from across the denominations in the same area.

And finally ...

Reaching out to children with the good news of Jesus is exciting and stimulating. Churches that are committed to this will have the joy of seeing children growing up in the church. They will also have stimulated and growing leaders. That's the effect evangelism has on the people leading it.

But the minister remains the person with the most significant role to play (whether or not children's evangelism happens is up to him or her). At the moment, there is little to encourage our busy ministers to take an active interest in what their churches provide for their own children or for those from outside.

If our denominations were to agree together on a syllabus of training for the early years of public ministry that included evangelism among children, what a difference it could make!

 Talk about it . . .

Questions for group debate or website:

- If a local church is struggling, how could we encourage development and growth?
- What role does a team of volunteers play in this process?
- How can a church be actively encouraged to 'think new'?
- You have prayed, planned and launched a new initiative affecting the whole life of the church. It doesn't work. How do you handle this apparent failure appropriately?

 You can continue this discussion by visiting the web on www.chancetochoose.com

Storybox 4
Scrappy puppet ensures smooth assemblies

Many ministers and church-member volunteers are invited to lead school assemblies. This is not an easy task, but John Fryer has turned assemblies into an art form. Commissioned by the Church of the Martyrs in Leicester, John's 'Primary Concern' ministry focuses on schools in and around the city. We can all learn from his approach.

I began leading Bible-based assemblies in primary schools in 1991, working with a local minister. I began to develop a method that not only brought the Bible into school in an exciting way but was also acceptable to staff, especially headteachers. As it transpired, it was acceptable to OFSTED inspectors too.

Being on school premises means that working within educational parameters is essential. I visit each school at least twice a term. Building relationships with staff and children ensures that my work is not a 'hit and run' assembly filler.

I acquired a puppet called Mr Scrappy, and he lives in a suitcase. Very soon I could see that this odd-looking character was accepted and loved. I noticed that the staff as well as the children listened when Scrappy had something to say, so

I added other puppets to my collection. Using them, I began to develop this pattern for my assemblies:

- Taking first the Bible story, I decide one thing I want the children to remember. For example, this might be obedience from the story of Jonah.
- Next, I work out a 'routine' with Mr Scrappy to illustrate the theme. For example, this might be that Mr Scrappy, despite being told, didn't put on his coat. Now he has a cold.
- Then I tell the Bible story in my own words (in an assembly I never read it straight out of the Bible).
- Finally, I try to show how this links in with what Mr Scrappy was doing earlier.

In some schools I use songs. This also reinforces the relevance of the message. Using acetates with bright pictures often helps the younger children to follow the story too. I am certainly not afraid to use humour. They love it. All this builds an assembly lasting between ten and fifteen minutes that is memorable and fun.

The key is to keep it simple. My aim is to enable children to have a positive experience of the Bible. Being able to dispel myths about church and Christianity is a wonderful privilege. If I can do that, then the assembly has been successful.

As one non-Christian headteacher wrote, 'It's Monday morning and into our assembly arrives John and his suitcase. After thunderous applause, a sea of faces comes to light; noise of eager anticipation is heard with expectant shuffling. We allow it, because we know that Mr Scrappy and John have a message from God. It will be one that we all like to hear and learn. The interaction is superb, the message clear and understood. The children enjoy it, even some staff! I wish I could do that with 400 children and I'm the Head!'

I picture the work this way. If you want an oak tree, it will take many years to grow, so you have to plant the acorn now. If you want a confident adult faith later, you have to start now. Children need to be given the building blocks of faith in their early years. Most parents no longer take their children to church or tell them Bible stories at bedtime, so it is vital that we find ways of filling that gap. We need to help them to see that these timeless stories show God was at work in history in our world. We want children to know that he still is and always will be at work in our world too. I always encourage children to read the Bible stories again, and with that in mind have linked with a Christian charity that gives grants to schools for buying Bibles and Christian books. This ensures that the children have access to God's word.

This approach obviously has impact. I have had older children, who have left primary school, come and chat to me on the street about assemblies they saw in the past. They always comment positively about them. I have lost count of how many teachers have personally thanked me for 'explaining that Bible story'.

Plant the acorns now. Trust and pray that God will water, nurture and grow the oak trees in the future.

5. So Much to Offer

Positive assessment of church resources

What fantastic resources the church has! We have every-thing we could possibly want readily available in order to contact children with the gospel. The church in our land is a huge resource of experience, pageant, celebration and festival. It has a history of all-age achievement and a vested interest in the future. In fact it has everything that should guarantee us acceptance and welcome with the new generation.

Well equipped

Let's list some of the many positive aspects that the church has going for it.

Man in the middle

At the centre of what we have to offer there is a person and a story. The two are impossible to separate. The person of

The church has so much to offer children.

Jesus Christ is central to the 'big story' of God that starts before the beginning of the world and finishes after the end of time. This man is a natural with children; they want to get to know him. Although the stories about him took place a long time ago in a distant part of the world, they still captivate the imagination.

The big story is one of unending love, compassion for the losers and care for the environment – winning against all the odds. At the heart of it is the promise of a world where the books will be balanced and injustice will finally end. Children love it! Encompassing everything, this big story is made up of lots of smaller stories, most of which are child-friendly. We have an ideal message for approaching children.

Valuable venues

Our huge buildings are magnificent to children. Oversized, hard to modify and impossible to heat, many of them are a perpetual headache for church authorities. But children love that which is enormous and different. They love the ornate and the ceremonial. Children think that echoing spaces and creaking floors are fun. Ancient pictures and artefacts fascinate them. They enjoy copying and touching and making rubbings. Church buildings are not a problem to most children – rather, they provoke questions and interest.

Meeting people is fun

Children love meeting people. They are curious about lives other than their own, and they do not have a problem with the people who belong to the church. They have many intimate questions they would like to ask.

Relationships are at the centre of a child's life. It is through relationship that they receive love, reassurance, information and structure. Of course, as we saw in Chapter 1, many of today's children have major struggles in this area. But their appetite for relationship remains strong.

The church is not a building with a handful of people in it now and then. The church *is* people, and relationship is a huge resource that we have on offer to a new generation.

Many different types of people make up the church. Some members are the same age as the children to whom we are reaching out, but there are many others who grew up in a very different time and culture. These people have achieved amazing things. They have brought up families, fought in a war, cared for sick people, made cars, won competitions, travelled overseas, grown their own food and baked their own bread. They are people a child would want to get to know. They have tried-and-tested abilities that a child would want to learn.

Though it's probably not about computers or space travel, these people are full of knowledge that would interest children. Many of them have time to talk about what they know – perhaps more than a child's parents or teachers might have. They want to talk about it too. Many of them belong to an era before television, when conversation was an accepted way of spending time. Such people grew up in families where discussion and debate were part of the normal way of life. These adults are happy to talk and to share their knowledge and thoughts.

God's people have many gifts and skills. Over the years some have gained considerable expertise. Some of the younger adults may have taken a 'gap year' between stages of education. They too have acquired skills, possibly in developing countries. Many church members have professional skills. Some have spare-time hobby skills. Some are creative. Others take part in sports or in environmental preservation. God's people are worth listening to and they are worth spending time with, just as other people are. Children can build interesting relationships with them.

Lots of fun

As well as a captivating message to tell, interesting buildings to use and fascinating people to get to know, the church has organisations that are especially for children to enjoy. Many of these are uniformed organisations offering opportunities to learn skills and enjoy activities in small groups. In them children start to learn independence and take their first steps in leadership. The range of activities available can be vast: camping and other outdoor activities; music-making; computer skills; sports; photography; video games and so on.

These organisations have much to offer children's leaders, as well as the children themselves. They can give support and training to leaders who are isolated or lacking confidence. Some of them arrange residential holidays for leaders to enjoy with the children from their group.

They often produce written resources and provide guidance on child protection policies or compliance with the Children Act. Some can offer advice on funding new projects. Others will know the best way in which to set up the new project when the funding has arrived. Many leaders have set up amazing projects with this kind of help.

Look back and wonder

The church has centuries of experience in finding innovative ways to communicate with an ever-changing scene. Evangelism is not a new way of thinking. People have written down their adventures in work with children. These books, many of them long out of print, form a fascinating and heartening insight into the way in which the church has risen to the challenge in past generations. Looking back is an excellent way in which to gain hope for the future.

So what's the problem?

What has happened to this store of rich resources? Have we exhausted the fund of captivating stories? What has changed? With so much at our disposal what stops us from

- throwing open our buildings;
- using our skills;
- getting to know children;
- giving children the chance to get to know us;
- offering our knowledge;
- broadcasting our story?

Let's try to identify some of the obstacles.

Believers who don't believe

Today there's a new phenomenon in the church: people who call themselves 'believers', but who actually do not believe. To be more precise, they are adults who, in practice, no longer believe in the church. They think that the church is irrelevant to the young. When it comes to the role of children in a place of worship, they are cynical. They do not believe that they, or the church, have anything to offer that children would find attractive. In fact some of them no longer believe the Christian faith, so they have little motivation for handing it on to a new generation.

So if we want the church to make an impact on children, we need to draw adult members into a new and life-impacting faith.

Members who don't belong

We also have an increasing number of people in the church who are members but do not truly 'belong'. Some are more committed to the building than to what it stands for. For example, if there's a move to alter the inside of an ancient church, such people will probably attend a weeknight business meeting, but they are far less likely to be in the church on Sunday to worship and to learn.

For others, it's simply a matter of time and priorities. For many people Sunday is now the day for visiting far-flung family members. Most people enjoy more holidays than formerly, so are away from home more often. In many cases, where church membership was once central to life, going to church is now something to do when there is nothing better on. For these people the disappearance of children from the church is not of major importance.

If we want children to have the chance to choose to live for God through Jesus, we need members who belong: people who will feel a profound sense of loss if children disappear from the church.

Messengers who don't give the message

Sadly, we have many people in the church who no longer talk about their faith. They may be happy to talk about many things – work, the neighbourhood, entertainment, the family – but they have difficulty in talking about their beliefs.

This means that children do not hear the voice of personal experience telling how Jesus has made a difference. They may well hear the Christian story explained in a school RE lesson by a 'neutral' teacher, but this does not have the same impact as hearing the gospel communicated by people whose lives are based on it. We need to free people from being tongue-tied about talking of what God has done for them.

The knowledgeable who keep their knowledge

Clergy and ministers are not the only ones in the church who are 'in the know' about the Christian faith. But too often we treat them as if they are the only source of such knowledge. There are many others who have a depth of Bible knowledge and understanding gained over many years. We should ensure that such people are encouraged and set free to share their knowledge.

The rich who keep their riches

There are many wealthy churches that never think of sharing their resources with those that are less fortunate. There is a widening gap between big (usually well-off) and small (often poor) churches. Big churches can usually call upon a wide range of talents and resources. They are often rich, both financially and in terms of talented people, but down their road, across their town or city, there are churches that need their help. The need might simply be for two extra people, or a piece of equipment, in order to start a group for children in that area.

We need big churches to see that sharing their wealth is a legitimate use of their resources, so that the kingdom of God will grow among the young.

Making a difference

Web wisdom

Let's share our knowledge and resources with one another as much as we can. There must be dozens of ways in which people concerned about children's work in a particular area could meet informally to talk and pray. And if pizza, beverages and the occasional cream tea can be built into the equation, so much the better.

In the last chapter I proposed linking children's leaders via a supportive website. It would be good to extend the site by linking it to a national database for all those involved in children's evangelism. This would provide a high-speed method of gaining information and swapping good practice.

With so much information available at the click of a mouse, the site would prove a valuable resource for prayer support. It would have the advantage of involving those unable to get involved in hands-on work, and it would give a breadth of 'prayer focus' going far beyond the needs of the individual local church.

Once fully operational, the site could help denominational leaders identify areas where plenty is going on for children, and also where little seems to be happening. Using it rather like the charts in a wartime 'ops' room, they could see that certain areas need support, and locate the churches that could possibly provide it, possibly via short-term training and encouragement.

The database would identify leaders according to their key skills. For example, you could click the mouse to draw up a list of gifted children's evangelists in, say, Northern Ireland. Another click and you would be able to identify all those skilled in training fellow leaders in Devon and Cornwall.

Training is top

In the present crisis, we need not only to find some answers but to ensure that the church is safe from such a crisis in the future. Our answers must include training a new generation of young people who are competent and fruitful in evangelism among children.

In the past some children's evangelists committed a large amount of time to training new leaders by the discipling method. In this approach, a single 'learner' works alongside an experienced evangelist who provides on-the-job training. Many of today's evangelists can point to people, long-retired, who discipled them to be competent in evangelism with children.

Unfortunately, not everyone is prepared to put so much time and effort into nurturing another's gifts and skills. The present situation demands that we offer training to groups of young men and women whose hearts God has stirred about the young.

Beacon centres

In Chapter 10 you will find details of some of the courses currently available, but we need more of them. We also need to increase the availability of small-scale, locally based training that has an informal slant.

How do we do this? Well, it should be possible to identify churches that are centres of excellence – places where children's evangelism is happening and which could act as resource and training centres for others. Some such churches have already been identified. How splendid it would be to have 'beacon' centres all over the UK and Ireland, readily accessible to all.

These centres would offer informal courses in church-based children's work and in children's evangelism. They could prove an excellent channel for disseminating good principles and good practice to a wide variety of churches. They would be a focus for support and encouragement. Many working in children's ministry are isolated and lonely, or struggling in small teams. A local centre would give access to a larger group, prayer support, stimulus and fresh ideas. People could swap stories of struggles and of joy.

Shared portfolio

The centres could form the basis of a national 'portfolio' of good practice. There are many ways of doing children's evangelism – no one method is right for all situations. Given time, we can sort out principles to work by and selection criteria for those who should be involved. When discouragement kicks in, when previously successful approaches go wrong, the portfolio could provide a rich source of ideas, information and discussion. It would help us nurture leaders who do not give up when things seem to be failing.

Above all, it would prove an antidote to that most damaging attitude of all, usually expressed with a sigh (or a cynical smile): 'Good idea, but it would never work *here*!' We need to encourage people to say, 'Well, if this doesn't work we'll try something else.'

Children in need

A database could help to identify those working with children at risk. This specialised work is increasing in its significance. The Child Poverty Action Group reported that on the day of the June 2001 General Election, 3.3 million children were living in poverty in the UK – one of the highest levels of child poverty in western Europe.[1]

These children need our complacent country to ensure that they have access to the warmth, clothing and food they lack. Our complacent church must ensure that they hear about Jesus too. The ability to contact – and link up – those involved in this ministry could help to promote high standards and good communication in this sensitive area.

---

[1] CPAG campaign newsletter, June 2001.

Where are you from?

Everyone's situation is different, but thinking in terms of different areas may help us to identify those where mutual help could be encouraged.

Outer housing estates. Many thousands of people live in the large public housing estates on the edges of our cities and towns. Many of these estates have the feeling of 'forgotten' places. Those who minister there often feel forgotten.

Birmingham-based minister Wallace Brown has written movingly of his years of service on an outer estate – the kind of no-go area that's dismissed by affluent outsiders as 'that place'.[2] Outer-estate children grow up believing they too are unimportant in the big social picture. Providing support for people working with these marginalised children in such areas should be a high priority.

The inner city. This area has its own challenges and rewards. The inner city can have a 'buzz' and a sense of history that's lacking on an outer estate. Many such places are now vibrant multicultural areas. The downside – pollution, decaying housing, vandalism and drug problems – can make people working with inner-city children feel isolated and alienated. They need links with others who can sympathise and share ideas with them.

---

[2] Wallace Brown, *Angels on the Walls* (Kingsway Publications, 2000).

In the 'burbs. Few people have much sympathy for suburban churches. With all their resources, they can appear complacent. But these churches need – and don't always get – support.

People often join these churches because they want to be anonymous; they don't want to get too involved. Those with children expect them to benefit from excellent resources. They would not necessarily want those resources made available for children outside the church. This kind of 'us first' attitude can make those involved in children's evangelism in these churches feel frustrated and isolated.

In the country. Finally, those who minister to children outside the church in rural areas have unique opportunities – and a unique set of challenges. Congregations tend to be small with a high proportion of retired people. It's often hard to find venues suitable for children's activities, and the need to provide transport can be a major problem. Leaders can often feel discouraged. Again, a website would give them access to others in rural areas for support and encouragement.

And finally . . .

Regardless of denomination, our church is rich in history, resources, buildings and people. That's plenty of fuel for optimism.

Of course we need to acknowledge the crisis that faces us. We also need to agree that God can use us to meet the challenge. I believe that the imaginative use of modern communication could be of tremendous benefit. By linking people together over the Internet, common needs can be recognised and solutions shared.

We need to look at the tough areas of the country where children are growing up and ask ourselves, 'How should people of faith respond to these situations? How can we approach these children with our wonderful message? How can we introduce them to Jesus?'

God cannot fail – we need to find out what he has on his mind for our tough places, and to support those who are his human tools there.

 Talk about it . . .

- How can we help church members who have a negative view of the church?
- Suggest some ways of encouraging greater commitment in members – without scaring them away.
- How can a church enable its members to share their faith with family and friends?
- Some church members have a great store of Bible knowledge and faith experience. How can we help them to share these riches with others?
- In our increasingly busy world, how do we encourage and develop volunteer leaders to help pass on the faith to children?

 You can continue the discussion by visiting the web on www.chancetochoose.com

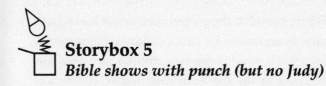

Storybox 5
Bible shows with punch (but no Judy)

Charlotte Nobbs uses puppet shows in the style of Punch and Judy to retell Bible stories to very young children at schools and playgroups. The technique has proved popular and successful. As well as being a home-based mother of four, Charlotte is involved in the children's work at St Giles, Northampton. She tells us how she started, and what has happened.

As a mum of pre-school children, I wondered how we could tell small children outside the church about Jesus. I'd seen children captivated by puppets and knew that everyone loves a good story.

With Christmas just a few months away, I asked local playgroups and nurseries if they would be interested in a Nativity puppet show aimed at under-5s. The responses were overwhelmingly positive. One playgroup leader replied, 'Oh yes! We don't want to do Santa this year – we want to do Jesus!'

A team of mums with young children met to plan this. Although none of us had experience of puppetry, we felt God wanted us to do it. Our aim was to be clear and focused – to tell Jesus' birthday story. We felt it important not to charge a fee. This was a Christmas gift from our church.

I wrote a script based on the gospel accounts of Jesus' birth in a way that was accessible for small children. For instance, 'Jesus is God's boy' included nursery rhymes like 'Twinkle, twinkle *great big* star' as the wise men follow the star to Bethlehem. The children were encouraged to greet the puppets. They knocked at the inn doors, and blew out the candles on a birthday cake for Jesus. I included plenty of repetition and encouraged interaction.

The puppets appeared in a Punch and Judy style box theatre. A narrator outside the set told the story, as I'd seen children uneasy without an observable adult in charge at Punch and Judy shows.

An artistic friend designed the simple, very inexpensive puppets. Experience has now taught us that it is best to prepare with all the puppet-makers working together. This brings uniformity in style, and tips are easily shared.

I recruited people through asking individuals to do specific tasks and through notices in church. Someone made the backdrops of a starlit night and an angelic scene. Someone else produced the front drop of the Bethlehem stable. Others made the individual figures and cattle that would be velcroed to the front drop as the show progressed. A cabinet-maker designed and made the theatre. It was built to be easily dismantled and assembled, and could be transported in an estate car. Others made the star-shaped biscuits we all shared at the end of each show.

Home groups prayed. They cut out card stars with

'Christmas is Jesus' birthday' written across them. This enabled each child to make a Christmas tree decoration at the end of the show. Members of the music group recorded a simple backing to accompany the songs.

There were three people in each production team:

- The narrator, who told the story standing outside the set.
- The puppeteer, who operated the movements of the puppets.
- The voice, who spoke for the puppets and handled scene changes, tape recorder and so on.

The teams rehearsed together and practised assembling the theatre. A production triplet presented the show at rehearsals to the other production triplets, modelling the show from the front and the back, and videoing it for subsequent review. The members then went home to practise behind their sofas!

We shared ideas on how to be as professional as possible. This included setting up promptly, being safe and being courteous to our hosts. We also practised assembling the theatre during the rehearsals.

I gave my last church notice for the puppet shows the night my daughter Emma was born, and three weeks later we were on the road.

It was an astonishing experience to witness children and their carers hearing Jesus' story, often for the first time. Many referred to the angel Gabriel as 'the fairy'. They sang the songs with enthusiasm, and waved and shouted 'hello' at the puppets. Many playgroup leaders commented how much their children enjoyed the shows. Children we knew were able to recount the Christmas story in a new way.

So, could the puppet shows be considered a success? Well, the story was well received. If a story is told well, the hearer will mull it over and return to it. Our outreach has now spread into schools and we are asked to present other biblical stories.

After one such production a woman told me she was not a Christian, but her son had seen our show. She and her partner felt it was right to retell the story to him 'as one day he might want to become a Christian'. We carry on, and let the stories of Jesus speak for themselves.

6. Strongest Links
Looking at the big picture of children's evangelism

So why pick out children as being special? Children are a vitally important part of any local church, but so is everyone. The exciting (and frustrating) aspect of the church is that it is for all: men, women, the old and the young, all races, the able-bodied and the disabled, the sophisticated and the simple, the educated and the illiterate, the bright and the challenged. Praise God that there is a valid place for all of us in our local church!

And yet children *are* special. They are the foundation of all that is to come. If the local church has an 'exclusive' membership (only white, only middle class, only female) then the church community is impoverished.

But if it is exclusively adult, it is not merely impoverished. Without the present-day colour, freshness, noise, hubbub, perception and special wisdom that come into the church with children, it is moribund. It has no future. What we invest in the young vitally enriches today's church. It will also provide the leadership in the church when we are no longer alive.

All-inclusive

The all-age church is exciting. It is not always the big churches (so-called 'family churches') that have healthy children's work. Size is less important than a strong emphasis on the all-age nature of the church.

Such churches will make their big decisions with all age groups in mind: from babies to centenarians. People will relate to one another across the age groups for the simple reason that 'good relating' should be natural to God's people. People will encourage one another to develop and maintain an all-age attitude. This will affect decisions about budget, use of rooms and choice of activity – in fact the overall strategy for the church.

Of course, not everything will be for everyone! Church life would be appalling if it became one long all-age service! The all-age church acknowledges that different age groups have different needs, but it also believes that we do not need to wait for children to grow up in order to become important. Each age group is as important as the rest.

An all-age church will gain a reputation in the community because of its unusual attitudes. This is one of the distinguishing marks of the life of God's people – the church sets a distinctive pattern of valuing *all* people, in contrast to our highly partial culture. Many people have come to faith and joined the church because members of the church community have given them a sense of personal worth.

Of course, a sense of self-worth is fundamental to helping children go out into the community as secure and confident individuals. The community to which they belong will have nurtured their beliefs and attitudes naturally. They will have been led and taught there by people they know well. They share in the lives of those older and younger than themselves. They see faith in action in their church community and are a vital part of it. Living as a member of a community of faith is fun – and hard work.

All-age community

This way of 'being church' requires a lot of continuous effort. It involves a work of God's grace to change the attitudes of a group of people from thinking about themselves to thinking about one another. That's the only way to achieve an all-age church. It usually starts when the leaders of the church adopt this 'others first' attitude.

Attitudes start to change when a church begins to look at its strategy for the next three, five or ten years. This is the starting point for an all-age church. There's no point in planning a strategy and subsequently asking, 'So what will we do with the children?' Such planning will include all age groups and people groups right from the beginning. (It's better to adopt a 'rolling' strategy that can be reviewed and adapted, as this makes for creativity rather than providing a straight-jacket.)

This calls for an excited, hopeful belief in the church. Local church leaders need to believe that God has good things for the church, and that he will do great things through the church for people of all ages. Church members need to hear them teaching the Bible with authority, particularly on the subject of the church. We need a renewed understanding of the church as the body of Christ: it grows as God blesses its obedience; it nurtures people of all ages.

At this point two issues become very important. One is the ongoing growth of a healthy church. The other is the development of gifts for evangelism among people of all ages. How much of this is happening in the church across the different denominations today? What is noticeable is a growing concern about all kinds of evangelism. Maybe the recent statistics have been heard.

Evangelist James Lawrence developed the innovative Lost for Words evangelism training course, and wrote a book with the same title.[1] He says, 'There's a growing number of adults who want to be confident in sharing their faith and who want to train others to be confident.' Many have now benefited from Lost for Words training, and have returned to their own churches with a course file, equipped to train others.

An all-age community including adults trained in faith-sharing means the picture's looking good, but it is still not complete for reaching out to children effectively.

---

[1] James Lawrence, *Lost for Words* (CPAS/Monarch, 1999).

Spot the difference

Children are different from adults and an understanding of the differences is important. Two specific areas need exploration: the child's spirituality and the child's faith.

Spirituality

A child's spirituality is not a poor version of an adult's. Quite the opposite in fact, as our spirituality can become jaded and sluggish as we grow older. A child appreciates colour and form. He is moved by beauty in people and landscape. She sees shape and beautiful movement in smoke and steam. He finds his own movements stimulating in dance and swimming. She finds deep satisfaction in supporting a football match with enthusiasm. He will stop and watch a snail or a ladybird. She will listen to the wind in the trees. She will stroke flowers and bushes. (Sadly, for many, difficult circumstances can close the door on this aspect of childhood experience. We mourn for the childhoods that should have been.)

Responses such as these are evidence of spiritual awareness. They may not be immediately obvious in the children around us, but if we give them opportunity for expression in conversation, we shall find them. (David Hay and Rebecca Nye[2] have been significant for many of us in the last few years in reintroducing us to the spirituality of the child.)

---

[2] David Hay and Rebecca Nye, *The Spirit of the Child* (HarperCollins, 1998).

123

Faith

When we introduce a child to faith, it is as if we are providing shoes for their spiritual feet. A child's feet will grow, regardless of whether they have the right size shoes. They will grow even if they have none. But if their shoes are the wrong size, their feet will be malformed. If they have no shoes they will have blistered feet. So when we introduce faith to children, we have to make sure we are getting the size right. If we provide an adult faith that is too big, or a patronising baby version, their 'feet' will be sore or malformed.

Recent years have seen a considerable amount of study with regard to faith development as it affects children. Two books are particularly helpful: *Christian Perspectives on Faith Development*, edited by Jeff Astley and Leslie Francis (Gracewing Fowler Wright Books, 1992) and *How Faith Grows* (Church House Publishing, 1991).

People learn in a variety of ways. Choosing the appropriate learning style is important when working with children – in fact, it's important with people of all ages. Marlene LeFever[3] has helped people grapple with this big issue.

What can we do?

All of this might sound rather a tall order. How can change be brought about in a way that is radical without being explosive? Here are some points that could help plot a safe

[3] Marlene LeFever, *Learning Styles* (Kingsway Publications, 1995).

path for a local church which is good news for children, even though it may not be large or making big news nationally.

Make an assessment

Begin with an 'audit' of your church at the moment. Look at the people you have, the buildings you use, the resources you own. Walk around the area your church serves. Try to look at it as if you have never seen it before. Talk to people working in the community. Ask them about the needs of the neighbourhood and their view of the church. Listen to church members from different age groups. Don't simply use 'thinking' terminology; ask them about their feelings, experiences and dreams.

Look at your finances

A financial check-up should be included in the audit process. Leaders will need to look at the level of finances, and at the trends detectable in the balance sheet. How are resources being apportioned? What proportions are being spent on the various age groups and on all-age provision? How much goes on maintenance matters, and how much is directed to mission? In particular, what is the difference between the proportion spent on evangelism and that spent on nurture?

Track the effectiveness of teaching and training

It is helpful to check out the effectiveness of the church's teaching for its members. What impact is it having on their personal growth, their development of new gifts and their take-up of new opportunities?

Here is an exercise for church leaders. Choose ten church members of various ages and backgrounds. Try to trace their 'development pattern' in the church over, say, the last five years. What jobs have they done? Which services, groups and events have they attended? To which aspects of church life do they contribute?

This kind of sample view should help with assessing what is happening across all the age groups. It will help with decisions on how to break into the life of the church in order to effect change. This could be with the aim of developing as an all-age community, or of becoming more effective in all-age evangelism – or of preparing to focus on children's evangelism.

Without this kind of audit, there is the risk of any new work simply being added on, not an integral part of the life of the church. This will cause problems for the leaders, who will not feel supported. It will cause even bigger problems for the people reached through these new efforts. They will have no obvious bridge into the main life of the church, whether they are children or adults.

Children's work – completing the puzzle

All-age edge

The various areas of work among children fit together like pieces of a jigsaw puzzle. The 'edge pieces' are all to do with the all-age nature of the church. Anything that explores and celebrates 'all-age' is an edge piece – social events as well as services, outings and spring-cleaning days.

Sunday school shake-up

All the other pieces belong on the inside: fit them together to complete the picture of children's work in and through the local church. Careful, creative provision for the children already in the church will account for many of the puzzle pieces. This has been the traditional activity of the church. Although it began with purely educational aims, the Sunday school system has, over the course of time, become one of the main ways in which children have been introduced to the church across the majority of the denominations.

Unfortunately, the tradition has not aged gracefully. In many cases it has retained a format and atmosphere from Victorian times. The energetic exploration of faith has not been one of its distinguishing marks. It has not been seen as a place where the Bible must be handled with care. Not surprisingly, when the approach to faith is repressive or boring, children vote with their feet.

Many churches, however, have given their Sunday groups a much-needed shake-up. They have adopted a child-focused approach and have had the courage to believe that children can engage enthusiastically with the Bible. An increasing number have taken the step of moving their 'nurturing' groups from Sundays to midweek. They have opened them to include children who have no family links with the church. This has been effective in terms of numbers. Children have come enthusiastically to groups that reflect their energy and their interests. They have found these groups to be places to which they can invite their friends without embarrassment.

Here is a list of key questions for a children's group health check:

- What is the aim of the group?
- Is it achieving its aim?
- If the aim is nurture of the church's children, is it achieving it?
- Are they learning about God and his word?
- Are they being given opportunities to worship God through Jesus?
- Are they experiencing God the Holy Spirit as they do so?
- Is the group aiming for them to 'become mature' (Ephesians 4:13)?
- How do the children react when their non-church friends come to the group?
- Do their friends respond well to the group?
- Do they feel that it is not meant for them?
- Do they feel they are being expected to believe without first finding out what they are believing in?
- Are you trying to do both nurture and evangelism in the same group?
- If so, are you experiencing success?

All-age services

Let's go back to the edge pieces and look at the benefits of a group of children getting involved in all-age services and contributing to the worship of the whole church. Such involvement gives them the chance to invite members of their family to come to church. The service gives non-church members of the community an excellent opportunity to be part of God's worshipping people. They don't have to pretend they believe in order to have a valid reason for being present. They can hear the truths of the Bible explained in language they can understand. They don't need previous experience. They can see what kind of group the child who has invited them has joined.

Parenting groups

Let's add some further pieces to the puzzle, pieces that are often ignored: groups to help adults explore parenting skills. Such groups can provide an important part of the picture. They have the advantage of bringing people together who share a common concern, regardless of whether or not they have Christian commitment. A parenting skills group can provide an area of trust where faith can be explored and known.

There's an extra benefit for the child whose parents, until this moment, have had minimal contact with the church. For example, suppose Tim's mum and stepdad have started going to the parenting group. Tim can breathe a sigh of relief. He is no longer his family's sole link with the church – the pressure is off.

Church leaders used to say that if they reached a child, they reached a whole family. This seems to place an unnecessarily high expectation on the child. Undoubtedly as children grow in their beliefs, their parents will notice. But why not reach the parent too and give the children some support along the way?

Celebrate the festivals

The next puzzle piece is our celebration of the various festivals of the church's year. Of course, the number and style of celebrations will vary according to traditions, but it is still worth considering how important these times can be. Each one gives the local church the opportunity to make known part of the Bible narrative. The community gets a chance to see the church as a worshipping congregation. The church members can meet people from the community while they 'party'.

The special millennium celebrations of Pentecost 2000 had a memorable impact on many communities. So why not make the message and meaning of Pentecost visible to those outside the church every year? The same goes for Easter and, perhaps to a slightly lesser extent, Christmas. Festivals also provide good openings for visiting schools to explain what Christians believe.

Evangelism

Next come the pieces that fill in the picture of focused evangelism among children in the community. Such events should be planned into the church's overall programme of children's work and evangelism. They must not be seen as something that happens haphazardly now and again because people feel guilty or dutiful.

The invitation lists will include children who have been

contacted through the year via a variety of aspects of the church's life. Church families will be encouraged to bring along friends of their children who do not belong to the church. Possible events include a sports event, a Christian pantomime, a mission event held over consecutive days, a regular club or a holiday club. The timing and content of the events should reflect both the social life of the children in the community and the availability of the church members who will be running them. Both are important.

Ownership

A programme of events could form an annual cycle as part of a strategy for children's evangelism that is agreed and owned by the whole church. As the church year proceeds, all the church members will be aware of what is happening and will be committed to praying.

In many churches responsibility for children's work is held by a small group of dedicated people. They are the ones who plan it, run it and pray for it, whether it is for nurture or evangelism. That's good, but what's better is the situation where the whole church is aware of what is going on and shares the sense of ownership, even though not everyone will be actively involved in the work.

With good planning it would be possible to distribute an annual programme outlining the work with children for the year ahead. It would be helpful for those actively involved and it would provide a splendid reminder for people providing prayer support or looking out for potential recipients of invitations.

Putting it together

Make a specific decision about how to complete the puzzle. (Perhaps this book so far has made you feel as if your puzzle is being *unmade* piece by piece.)

When a church begins to look with renewed vision at its ministry with children, it is important to look at all the options; to spread out all the pieces of the puzzle. Take a good look at them and begin by putting together the edge pieces, the all-age church. What next? Here is a suggested order for putting the puzzle together:

- All-age church – specific people with responsibility for this.
- Teaching – whole-church Bible teaching about the all-age nature of the church, the value of young and old, the meaning of the festivals.
- Festival celebrations – small planning group for these.
- Other all-age services – another small planning group.
- Nurture of Christian children – home groups, Sunday groups, email groups.
- Links with local schools – assemblies, RE lessons, school visits to church buildings, prayer support for local school staff, volunteer help for the school from church members.
- Children's evangelism – clubs, mission, weekly or monthly days out, summer camps.
- Parenting groups – mutual support, training, evangelism.
- Training – for church leaders.
- Training – for nurture leaders, evangelism leaders, all-age leaders.

We're learning lots *on our summer camp – wish you were here!*

Once again, I emphasise the importance of training for all involved. Training ensures that God has an effective tool in his hand. Leaders in churches with few resources and little money would probably hesitate before approaching a training organisation. They should go ahead and contact them anyway to ask them about how they could help and, possibly, to negotiate with them about their fees.

The solution may be for a group of churches to combine to share the costs of a training event or series of events. Large, well-resourced churches could invite other churches to share in their own training events – a generous use of resources, and a positive way of developing good relationships between local churches.

And finally ...

All of these ideas and suggestions aim to help break the silence surrounding this aspect of the life and ministry of many churches. There may be hundreds of children who would enjoy the corporate life of your church but who are excluded because there is no one to link them to you – no parent, grandparent or best friend at school who has a relationship with the living God. So they never hear about God and they do not know how to come to him through Jesus. That is not fair!

Every child has a right to hear and to make up their own mind. They cannot do that until churches choose to include outreach to such children in their overall strategy.

 Talk about it ...

How can we help develop adult understanding of how children believe?

- Fred says, 'I'd love to help with the children's group, but the generation gap is simply too big.' How would you encourage Fred to go ahead?
- How can we encourage a 'can do' attitude to children's evangelism in the face of disillusionment in the church?
- What would be a good first project to ensure a taste of success for a church trying new ways of reaching out to the young?

- What would you do to assess the most appropriate starting point for children's evangelism in the local church?

 You can continue this discussion by visiting the web on www.chancetochoose.com

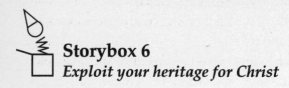

Storybox 6
Exploit your heritage for Christ

Nick Harding, Schools Officer at Southwell Minster, runs the award-winning 'Time Travelling!' experience for some 8,000 children a year. Since its start in 1995, some 45,000 children have taken part. But don't let the numbers put you off. Read what Nick does, and note his final comments. The principle could work anywhere.

Time Travelling! began as a response to the need to share the message of Christianity with children. At the same time it developed Southwell Minster as an educational resource. Since then programmes for the National Curriculum's Key Stages 1 and 2 have been developed and expanded.

Time Travelling! bookings open a year ahead. It is usually full eight months before the March fortnight for 7–11s and the June week for 5–7s. The cathedral is taken over by the project and most other regular activities take place elsewhere.

Time Travelling! Activity Days begin with the children arriving in groups of about twenty. They meet their volunteer guide who escorts them through the day. Guides are dressed in medieval pilgrim costumes and are encouraged to be the light of Christ for the pupils, however challenging they may be!

After processing and chanting through the great west doors the day opens with worship. This is key to the whole experience. As the day begins, children are encouraged to pray, think, sing and reflect.

Then each group follows an individual route and takes part in up to seven activities. These range from finding out about the building itself to thinking and praying. Activity Base Leaders guide the children through the significance of objects and places such as the font, pulpit and altar. In the process they share their own faith. Other activities are based round craft. Groups make angels, rub brasses and draw gargoyles. Some are even more practical like playing the organ or being involved in drama. Some children explore the churchyard.

The Activity Day always ends with worship. This again combines quiet for prayer and reflection with stories and activity. At the end each school is presented with a candle to take back as a reminder of the light of Christ. Each child receives a certificate to commemorate the pilgrimage experience. They also take back a leaflet explaining more about the Christian faith.

Each Activity Day relies on the help of at least eighty-five volunteers. They are drawn from a team of 320 people willing to be trained and assessed. They give up their time to work on this project. Clergy and laity, they are drawn from a range of church backgrounds and denominations. They are united in the aim of sharing a little of their faith with children. All team members attend a commissioning service and there are at least two training sessions for them. They are given specific roles for each day.

Many schools include Time Travelling! in their curriculum. It provides them with cross-curricular materials that are clearly Christian to prepare pupils for the Activity Day. Classroom books contain lesson plans, worksheets and assembly outlines. These can be supplemented by using a video and education pack on the minster. Laminated photo packs and audio tapes of songs and stories are also available. Local clergy are actively encouraged to go into schools and prepare them for their visit.

Time Travelling! has made a significant mark on the two Local Education Authorities. We have welcomed 300 schools so far, as well as churches throughout Nottinghamshire and beyond. Evidence shows that children, teachers and parent helpers have all been touched by their experiences at Time Travelling! The team prays that the work of the Holy Spirit in them will last.

In 1998 one child wrote this prayer: 'Dear God, thank you for letting me come to your house today. Please help Mummy and Daddy stop fighting.' If that boy is the only one who has been touched by God, then even that is enough.

Many smaller churches in the diocese now hold days for local schools based on the Time Travelling! model. Others have found that Time Travelling! has given them a foot in the door of schools in order to build stronger relationships. This highly organised and intensive approach really works.

But this is true not only on a large scale with many children and volunteers. It is true also in any local church with a few willing people and a little forethought. All churches have resources to use as a springboard for teaching and sharing. This should always be more than an educational visit. It is an opportunity to demonstrate the love of God through what is said and done, allowing the children to hear the message of Christ.

7. Adult Concerns

Including the older generation

Adults, as well as children, can fix themselves in the memory. I remember clearly the woman who brought me to the point where I could 'own' my faith for myself. Her name was Daphne Johnston and she led camps for teenage girls on behalf of the Africa Inland Mission. I haven't seen her since I was about sixteen, but I'll never forget her.

People of influence

For most of us who came to faith in Jesus in our childhood, an adult was involved. Adults are powerfully influential in any child's life – so powerful that children either fight against them or take them as their role models. This poses an enormous challenge for any children's leader. How do we use such influence with integrity? How do we ensure that we are not simply growing our own group of adoring followers?

This question of influence is of even greater concern in evangelism with children. We want children to come to know Jesus through coming to know us. We want them to have a personal relationship with him because they have one with us. We have to guard against the danger of being too influential or too persuasive. Going too far in that direction could prove a hindrance to their growing relationship with God.

All leaders are seen as 'grown-ups' by children, regardless of the size of the age gap between child and leader. As leaders, we need to recognise that difference. We shall never be a child growing up in the twenty-first century. Some leaders of children's groups are young themselves. They may be in their teenage years or early adult life – young and gifted people who are very attractive to children. They exert, usually unconsciously, a strong influence on them. But to children the leader is still in a world apart.

Facing the difference

The age gap is also an experience gap. The word 'different' needs to ring in the ears of any children's leader. We need to face the challenge of working with people who are different from ourselves – children.

A leader may see the relationship between adult and child as representing 'right and wrong', or 'wise and naïve', or 'give and receive'. If so, the relationship, whether for nurture or evangelism, will not be as it should be. The key fact is that a child's world is different, and the leader has the responsibility to get to know that world.

Learning across the generation gap.

Most churches have a problem finding enough leaders for children. This is one reason why many churches have little appetite for reaching out to children outside the church – they do not *want* more children in the church. If more arrived, they would bring with them the need to find more leaders.

But why is there this reluctance to work with children? The world of the twenty-first-century child is fascinating. The company of children is exhilarating as well as demanding. The learning needed in order to lead children is stimulating to personal faith. Why do few adults have the appetite for this? There are several reasons.

142

'I'm already doing enough'

Lacking a strategy for ministry, many churches have to use one adult for more than one role. As some congregations dwindle, the strategy of the church is not rethought. The faithful few collect more and more jobs. Concentrating on church-focused maintenance, they have little contact with people outside the congregation.

At the same time, secular employment is becoming more precarious and more demanding. Those in employment can no longer presume that simply doing their job will keep them employed. They need to work harder. They need to be noticed for being more committed than their colleagues.

Few people now have a lifelong career. Some of their job changes are brought about by redundancy. Some changes require further education or training. With these economic factors comes personal stress. With this kind of pressure, it is not surprising that many are 'not available' to help at church.

Employment pressures can also cause a gender imbalance in children's leadership. I have already noted the encouraging development of midweek groups for children, many of them with an emphasis on evangelism. They often take place late in the afternoon, before the end of the working day. It is usual for men to work further away from home than women. Mothers are more likely to be the carer than fathers. So midweek groups not only struggle to find leaders, they are rarely able to find a male leader. So boys at midweek groups are likely to have solely women as their role models.

'It's a waste of time'

Running a good children's club or activity is a challenge – it takes commitment. If it's a midweek set-up, the children arrive after a busy day at school, mentally tired but with plenty of physical energy. They will be hungry, ready for more than a drink and a biscuit. They will be thoroughly familiar with each other after a day at school and some may be in the mood to continue playground arguments or fights. The children will probably come from more than one school and the club requires them to 'gel' into one group.

What do the leaders have to provide? Not much, really! They have to deliver a club that's fun and has good discipline, where good relationships are being built between leaders and children and between the children themselves. They need to 'shape' the club experience so that the children come back week after week. Most of all they have to ensure clear communication of what they want to say.

There's no getting away from it: achieving these aims *is* hard work. At the end of some sessions, leaders will look back in dismay on the perpetual struggle for discipline. Many times they will think despairingly about how the talk has been received, or about how the activities related to it have gone. Sometimes they will watch children going home still caught up in the arguments they brought with them from school. They will ask themselves whether it has all been worth it. Sometimes it will be very difficult to believe that it has been.

'We've said all this before'

Adults have the gift of memory and experience. There are some in every church who have led children's groups faithfully over many years. They may well look back on years of telling children about God's love, and reflect on the invitations they have given to children to come to know him. They may look among their own congregation for people to whom they spoke about Jesus years ago, and not find them there. And they struggle to believe that their message has any impact. Perhaps it is too out of date to impress the young culture.

'We've tried all this before'

It's not only the message that can seem faded. So can the messengers. People can be in children's leadership for too long. Many remain vibrant and enthusiastic despite advancing years, but sadly some can blight new ideas: 'We tried this before, and it didn't work then.' Nothing is more damaging to the faith and enthusiasm of newer leaders.

Some of us *have* been around for a long time and we need to stop and ask God whether we should continue in work with children. Maybe he wants us to move into different roles – he never makes us redundant. An older, experienced leader would perhaps make an excellent leader of a group of people praying for the club.

'It wasn't like this when I was a child'

It certainly wasn't! This attitude brings us back to the key message: we need to get to know the culture of the child as intimately as possible. Spending time reading their comics and magazines, watching their programmes, listening to their music, visiting their schools will pay dividends. Making time for home visits will also be an important aspect of the group leader's commitment.

The Hezekiah attitude

There's a prevailing attitude in today's church that is mirrored in the closing scene of the life of King Hezekiah (2 Kings 20:12–21). Hezekiah has entertained the envoys of an ungodly neighbouring kingdom. He has been bragging to them about his possessions and has shown them the extent of his power and the riches of his spoils. Isaiah the prophet comes to tell him what a fool he has been. He tells Hezekiah that ultimately his action will cause the fall of Jerusalem.

> Then Isaiah said to Hezekiah, 'Hear the word of the Lord: The time will surely come when everything in your palace, and all that your fathers have stored up until this day, will be carried off to Babylon. Nothing will be left, says the Lord. And some of your descendants, your own flesh and blood that will be born to you, will be taken away, and they will become eunuchs in the palace of the king of Babylon.'
> 'The word of the Lord you have spoken is good,' Hezekiah replied. For he thought, 'Will there not be peace and security in my lifetime?' (2 Kings 20:16–19)

Hezekiah listens to a prophecy of national calamity, involving even his own offspring, yet he applies the word 'good' to Isaiah's message. Why? Because the 'bad thing' will not happen in his own lifetime.

Hezekiah's attitude is alive in the church today. We can look at the situation in children's evangelism and recognise that millions of children are not being given the chance to make up their minds about Jesus. We can hear the consequent effect on the numbers of adult church members. Yet we can remain complacent because, like Hezekiah, we won't see the threatened 'meltdown' in our lifetime: 'Will there not be peace and security in my lifetime?'

A positive response

How should we respond to such a situation positively and creatively? How can we achieve the impossible and turn this situation round? And, taking the long view, how can we ensure that a future generation does not have the same problem in fifty years' time?

Perhaps we can find some answers by focusing on this book's primary concern: the children who never hear about Jesus. But we do not simply want them to hear about him – we want them to come to know him and to grow to spiritual maturity. How do we achieve that? Their growth in faith has eight different areas, all of which require attention.

Growing in understanding the Bible

We want children's faith to be strong and resilient. We want them to be in fellowship with other Christians, playing their part in the local church. Their faith needs to grow to independence so that they will remain faithful even when surrounded by antagonistic people. This aim won't be achieved by getting to know group leaders better or by having a better time in a club. It will be realised as they become increasingly able to receive from the Holy Spirit through reading the word of God.

The majority of children learn to read successfully. Most will cross the line where reading becomes a pleasure rather than an effort. Leaders should come alongside this process with the Bible. There is an excellent choice of modern translations. Several organisations provide attractive notes and booklets to help children to read the Bible every day. Some leaders have set up email groups to communicate with their members as they read short daily portions of the Bible together, and of course members can 'e-chat' with one another about the chosen passage.

Growing in personal faith

Generations of Christians have grown in faith as they feed daily from the Bible, although it is easier for others to see this happening in us than it is for us to measure it in ourselves. As the Holy Spirit applies the teaching of Jesus to our lives by his power, our nature changes into Christ's nature. This is God's lifelong work to prepare us for heaven. It gives us the strength we need for today and the hope we need for the future.

As we grow, our communication with God in prayer will become more urgent and more instinctive. Prayer is our lifeline. All of life's daily experience can find expression in it, and it is the means by which we can hear the voice of God speaking deeply, bringing us wisdom, encouragement and discernment.

This is true for children as well – in fact, children often seem to be better at listening to God than adults are. They are certainly more tenacious with their prayer requests. As a child's faith grows, he or she becomes more able to believe on behalf of others.

Growing in spiritual gifts

Children learn about spiritual gifts when they read the Bible, and from their experience in the local church. They will gain insights as they see spiritual gifts used in their group and in the wider church congregation. As with any other kind of upbringing, children are susceptible to adult example. They will watch and often mimic our attitudes and actions.

The gifts that are being used in their local church are likely to be the ones that new Christians will discover. But be ready for exceptions. God loves to surprise us through children who come to faith, and they are often the ones in whom God does something new. We need to be careful not to ignore what he is doing through children from families *outside* the church. They are often the ones who are most available for him to display his power in a new way.

Growing in the right environment

As children in a church-based club begin to come to faith, they will start to explore the Bible and display energy in prayer. They need an environment where they can enjoy this new life and grow towards maturity. To help them the church will have to be committed to providing ongoing nurture within the club, or to providing a special nurture group for them.

Problems can arise for the non-church child if the nurture group is full of children from church families. This may not be a suitable environment for new Christian children, and Sundays may not be the best time for children from non-church families to get to church. In fact, linking with church may simply prove to be very 'socially complicated'. In view of this, some churches are finding that the good way to nurture a small group of new Christian children is by forming an after-school home group for them, where they can enjoy the Bible, use their spiritual gifts and worship Jesus together.

Growing in ways of 'being church'

A good nurture group will build a bridge for children to cross to the main body of the church. This will probably be through the church's all-age activities. As well as being accessible to all age groups, these should provide access for people at different stages of faith. Established members should try to build relationships with new Christian children as they accept them joyfully into the church community.

Of course new children will bring changes as they start contributing to the life of the church. But some changes may be unwelcome, causing worry and discomfort, possibly more for older members than for other groups. While they will probably see the importance of change, they will need courage and energy to adapt to new situations. If they accept change, they will benefit from a healthier church, but they will have to be prepared to cope with the turbulence that change brings in its wake.

Growing in leadership

The gift of leadership is not limited to adults. Children can lead, and visiting any crèche will convince you of that fact. It is easy to pick out the 'born leader' as you watch small children interact with one another! But leadership is a gift of the Spirit and therefore is not limited to strong, 'natural' leaders. As children come to faith, we should pray that the Holy Spirit would give this gift to the church through them. We need leaders for today and for the future.

Children's groups, clubs and residential activities are ideal places where children's leadership skills can grow and be exercised. Children can take responsibility for specific areas of service. The important thing at this stage is that they should be given a safe, supportive environment in which to find their feet. As with any new leader, they must not be left in an exposed position where they could fail publicly. For example, the leader could ask a child to take responsibility for the names and concerns to be included in the group's weekly prayer list, and for leading the actual prayer time. This will involve some preparation, when the child discusses the task with an adult leader – both the prayer needs themselves and the ways in which people might be encouraged to pray. The leader will be sure to be present at the planned prayer time. Afterwards leader and child will meet for feedback. My recommended ratio for such feedback times is as follows: four specific encouragements to one 'Why don't you try to do such and such differently next time?'.

Growing as trainers

The church lacks people who are good at handing on their skills to others, which is another reason for our shortage of adult leaders. When children come to faith in our groups, we need to start to develop a trainer's attitude, encouraging them to think of themselves as people with skills that could be handed on to others.

The uniformed organisations set a good example in this area by encouraging children to work towards badges and awards. They identify key skills and develop enjoyable and original ways via which those who have already achieved them can pass them on. We need to acquire some of this attitude in our evangelism.

Regardless of whether they arrive from inside or outside the church, children who come to faith are whole people, not just souls! They have natural gifts and skills that God is going to nurture to equip his church. We should ask God to give us this 'whole person' attitude.

Our prayer as leaders should be that each child would become an active and contributing member of the church. We shall need to discern the gifts and strengths of each child and encourage the 'trainer attitude' in them to help them see that they have gifts and skills that others could learn from them.

Growing in evangelism

Adults know God and introduce children to the God they know. So goes our traditional pattern of children's evangelism – and there is nothing wrong with such an attitude. But it is not the complete picture. It would be more accurate to say that people know God and introduce people to the God they know. There is a huge difference between the two statements.

Adult emphasis:

- The adult introduces the child to Christ.
- The child responds.
- The adult moves on to the next child.

All-age emphasis:

- Anyone introduces anyone else to Christ.
- They see 'spiritual light' in a child.
- They encourage the child to speak out about his or her faith.
- They resource the child to introduce others to Christ.
- The child introduces anyone else to Christ (and we are back at the top of this list).

Children are natural evangelists, speaking about what has happened to them in 'un-churchy' language. They love to mull over spiritual thoughts out loud. These are ideal communication skills for evangelism. (There are countless stories of parents who have come to faith through the words and example of their children.) We should encourage the natural growth of this process and we should support children as they grow.

Sometimes talking about faith is hard work. Any of us can become discouraged. We all know the disappointment when the way we live lets down the message we give. Children are people. These things happen to them too. We need to support them by prayer and to be available to listen to them as they talk through their experiences. We want to grow them in evangelism. This will ensure that their generation will have confident people who can share their faith with others.

And finally ...

This chapter has highlighted the contrast between the church as it is and the church as it could be. We see the attitudes and aspirations of the generations that are already in the church. We see the children who could come to faith through us. We see the different ways that faith can be grown from its outset. We see the way in which we can have the vision for a new way of 'being church'. God is calling us to blaze a trail for children to find their way to Jesus. They can then lead the church into a brighter future.

 Talk about it ...

- How can we provide opportunities for children to read the Bible and to rely on it?
- How can we give opportunities for children to use spiritual gifts?
- How can we create opportunities for children to lead?

- How can we give opportunities for children to be evangelists?
- How can we make it possible for experienced children to train others?

 You can continue this discussion by visiting the web on www.chancetochoose.com

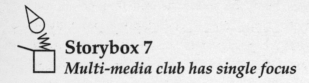

Storybox 7
Multi-media club has single focus

In eighteen months Club 2000 has reached over 250 children in Macclesfield with the message of Jesus, through a dynamic mix of music, games and Christian teaching. It is organised by Holy Trinity Church, Hurdsfield, and I asked Sue Warham, a head-teacher and member of the church, to tell me about it.

So what exactly is Club 2000?

Club 2000 is aimed at seven- to eleven-year-olds who have little or no previous knowledge of Jesus. The clear Christian teaching is presented in a fast-moving, multi-media format. The programme includes music, rules, memory verse, praise party, games, Bible story, object lessons, life application, story and prayer.

So far the children have learned about the Ten Commandments, the miracles of Jesus and some of the great Bible heroes. Each week, one single Christian truth is reinforced throughout the programme. The children are encouraged to apply this truth to their own lives.

Club 2000 attracts children from a range of backgrounds. Many face difficult situations. Some come from complicated family relationships. Some come with emotional and behavioural problems. Many have experienced frequent house moves, traumatic times and social deprivation. Others appear to have much greater stability. Yet all these children are keen to come. They want to have fun and they listen attentively to the Christian message. It's a privilege to get to know them. We receive personal invitations to school plays and we are greeted cheerfully when we meet them in town. We enjoy responding to their questions and requests for prayer.

How and why did you begin?

We knew we had to reach out to the children and young people of the local community, but didn't know how. During my monthly meetings for prayer with two other headteachers of church schools, we began praying for the schools we passed each day on our way to work. I passed the only school within the parish of the church I attended. I now know that God was preparing the ground for where we would soon begin the club!

Then I heard about the Kidz Klub in Liverpool (see Storybox 3). We visited it and were amazed at what was happening. Travelling on the collection buses around Toxteth we saw the sheer delight of children eager to come along. They sang their hearts out, whether it was loud rap or quiet worship. They clearly remembered the memory verses and Bible teaching from the previous week. The enthusiasm of the children and the large team was infectious. Something very special was clearly going on. Here was our God-given inspiration.

Our church was keen to hear about what God was calling us to do. I thought through every issue carefully, not wishing to jump on a 'band wagon'. I wanted to evaluate everything we had seen. We needed to question what would and wouldn't work. We needed to visit and appraise other children's activities in the area. We had to decide on an appropriate entry point.

We began to plan and prepare for the millennium launch of Club 2000. It was exciting to realise that others were also prepared for this opportunity. When we came together as a team of around twenty, we had all the range of skills we required!

Do you have contact with the children's families?

Yes. An important aspect of Club 2000 is the regular visits we make to see the children in their homes. This may be for a brief chat on the doorstep to hand over the week's newsletter and activity sheet, or it may be for a longer chat over a cup of tea, but these visits are a means of building one-to-one relationships. They also demonstrate that we care beyond the ninety-minute club.

We have continued to run our holiday Bible clubs and to work with local schools. This is particularly important so that the children meet us in their own environment. We also lead assemblies, encouraging the children to try out the club for themselves, by giving them a taster of the sort of things we do.

So where do you go next?

Over the last year the club has at least doubled in numbers. From a regular attendance of between thirty-five and forty children, we now have a regular attendance of between eighty and 100. One week we had 116! It is important that we continue to build deeper one-to-one relationships.

We must disciple those who have made a commitment. We must care for those who are almost ready to do so. We need to provide further opportunities to reach out to their families. We are also seeking to establish a team to take the children on through the teenage years.

8. Beyond the Boundaries
Co-operation across the denominations

A welcoming angel was showing a new arrival around heaven. The angel was reassuring and they chatted companionably. They arrived in one area near a high wall with a firmly closed door. Over the top of the wall came the sound of quiet voices. The angel signed to the new arrival to be very quiet until they had passed. Then the angel explained: 'We have to be quiet there. It's the Brethren and they think they are the only ones here.'

I was brought up in the Brethren, became a Baptist when I was a student, and subsequently married an Anglican in the independent evangelical church where I was a member. In marrying him I joined a Jewish family. The joke above did the rounds when I was a teenager in the Brethren. I'm sure it could still be told about any of us, from whatever denomination.

We all belong to one area or another of the church. Labels abound: charismatic, evangelical, conservative, liberal,

Anglo-catholic . . . Within each of those areas we belong to a variety of denominations. Each has its own culture, history and traditions, giving the whole church its rich diversity. Presumably each group thinks it is right – perhaps a bit more right than all the others.

Interdependent people?

Let's try to identify, out of this huge subject of children's evangelism, those issues that could be worked on if we all made the effort to think across denominational divides. There are people in every denomination who can take some responsibility for encouraging changes of attitude, and action. Unless this happens across the whole spectrum we will never turn the tide for children. The crisis is too severe.

Wake up

This is a national crisis. Some readers may ask what all the fuss is about. Possibly their children's groups are thriving. That's great – there are certainly places where new ideas have proved to be successful, and in some areas the church is making contact with an impressive number of their local, non-church children – but looking at the whole of the UK and Ireland, such advances are the exception.

For every child to have the chance to choose, we need to think nationally, not locally.

All involved

It is an interdenominational crisis. Researchers Leslie Francis and David Lankshear have identified where the losses are and they have also pinpointed where people are most successful at reaching and keeping their children.[1] Peter Brierley of Christian Research has given us a recent jolt with his statistics.[2]

Responsibility cannot be assigned to one denomination more than any other. Perhaps your own denomination is doing successful work with children in your area.

For every child to have the chance to choose, we need to think nationally rather than denominationally.

Diversity

This is a 'patchy' crisis. There are areas of the country where an individual church may have contact with only one child. In exceptional areas it is still fashionable to go to church. In other areas children hear nothing about Jesus because they live in communities where the majority of people are Sikhs, Hindus or Muslims. Or they simply live where Christians have become careless and complacent.

For every child to have the chance to choose, we need to think nationally, not regionally.

---

[1] *In the Evangelical Way* (National Society, 1995).
[2] *The Tide Is Running Out* (Christian Research, 2000).

Blind eye

The people who could make most difference to this crisis are those who find it easiest to turn a blind eye. They are also the people most likely to read a book like this. (Hello!)

You, like me, are probably able to choose where you live and work. We can also choose where we go to church. We may have the option of choosing to belong to a church that has a thriving children's ministry. Such a church will be healthy for our children and may offer effective outreach for our children's friends. But we are the exceptional people. As the shocking statistics prove, there are millions lacking our privilege of choice.

It is not enough to look at our own church and ensure that children have a chance to choose. We need to think nationally, not congregationally.

We need to change our thinking in these four ways because of our concern for the *whole* church – God's church. He commanded that we hand on our faith from generation to generation, not try to ensure the future of our particular denomination over any others.

Ecumenical events have traditionally struggled for support. People are committed to working hard in their own local church, but they often find it impossible to make the extra time for events linking them to other churches. The absence of strategic planning in the church is probably another cause of this lack of time and energy for inter-church links.

In any case, such links are rarely profitable. Sometimes they can simply provide a reason to have an extra service. They rarely offer the opportunity for viable outreach or sustainable children's work.

Small churches usually recognise that they need help and are often keen for partnership with other churches. Sadly, those who could provide help often suffer from complacency and self-sufficiency. Sometimes there is a competitive spirit around in large, thriving churches that can foster fear: if we give anything away, we may later be in need ourselves. Surely the truth is that God provides for us when we give things away. And isn't he likely to leave us to fend for ourselves when we clutch at our resources for our own use?

It is possible to be so inward-looking as a church that we remain unaware of the needs of other local churches. We could be much more open with one another about what we do, and far more curious about what God is doing in and through our neighbouring churches. Then we would be more aware of opportunities for giving and receiving help.

Most people dislike change. They are particularly opposed when it seems financially threatening. Giving equipment, money or people to a church across town from us or in a nearby village will be a costly sacrifice, but we need to see this as missionary giving. Thanks to a large church's generosity, children in a less well-off area can at last have a chance to hear about Jesus.

Such sharing challenges the 'Hezekiah attitude' to its core. It takes to heart the truth that when one limb of the body is sick, the whole body suffers.

Aiming for interdenominational agreement

Talk at the top

There is a desperate need for leaders of the main denominations and movements to spend time together talking about children's evangelism. (For generations we have limited such conversations to the children's 'specialists'.)

Direction-setting

There are leading 'voices' in each denomination that we are used to hearing giving teaching, opinion and prophecy. These authoritative people should include children in what they have to say. They should call the church to action and challenge our complacency, taking the lead in encouraging us to pray for children. Direction should be set from the top in each denomination or movement.

Help with theology

Our leaders should get together to think through the theological issues surrounding children coming to faith. The aim would be for open, honest discussion of those areas of doctrine and belief that most affect those approaching children with the gospel, rather than leaders becoming more entrenched in their views, or sponsoring interminable discussions about whether children are 'out until they opt in' or 'in until they opt out'.

It would be good, for example, to have guidance on some of the following topics:

- Does God's view of the children of Christian parents differ from his view of the children of non-Christians?
- How much does a child have to understand in order to belong?
- How much does a child simply have to receive in order to belong?
- What are the possible entry points for children into the church?
- What new rites of passage would be helpful and biblically appropriate in order to welcome children?
- If we don't practise infant baptism, then when is a child old enough for baptism?
- How do we account for the variety of practice affecting children and Holy Communion?

The church should celebrate her variety and acknowledge her disagreements, but surely we also need to be led by people who are prepared to discuss both openly? Those of us grappling with evangelism among children need the benefit of their reflections and discussions.

Small can be beautiful

Big isn't always best. We need this acknowledgement from our leaders across the denominations. The good news stories about outreach usually emerge from the big congregations, which is not always helpful.

Any church, however small, can open its doors to the young, can make provision for them and can get involved in evangelism. This attitude needs denominational backing.

Denominational leaders should encourage churches, large and small, to co-operate.

Faith is the key

National denominational leaders should encourage churches to provide overt teaching on the way of faith for all ages, clearly advocating the validity of lively faith in child-hood. This would encourage churches of whatever persuasion or structure to make that provision. They should speak against the 'child-minding' attitude of our churches. The church exists to make disciples of all ages, and we need encouragement from the top to make this happen.

Shared welcome

At the moment some children in our churches are welcomed, but others are made to feel in the way. Others – millions of them – have never been inside a church at all. The church should offer a common voice of welcome to all our children. Our denominational leaders must make welcoming children a high-profile priority, something they endorse *together*. This national voice of welcome must be heard even by those outside the church.

Summit meeting

Let's call for a 'summit meeting' of denominational and other leaders with national influence. It could form the basis of a new approach to sharing resources for training, and for the staffing and financing of projects.

Take the following as an example of the kind of practice

that a new common approach could influence. At present some churches use the stipulations of the Children Act (and other legal requirements) as an excuse for being unable to make provision for children. One can almost hear the sigh of relief: 'Sorry, but we simply can't meet the legal demands.'

We need our leaders to show solidarity of concern and purpose, so that no church is able to make such excuses. With a common approach on the sharing principles of evangelism, the provision of legal guidance and other practicalities, there could be new impetus for getting on with the task of reaching children.

Consider the situation in the church described in the early chapters of Acts. The believers shared their possessions so that no one was in need. Today's denominations could do the same. The result could be as exciting now as it was then: 'The Lord added to their number daily those who were being saved' (Acts 2:47) – 3,000 in one day!

If our national leaders were regularly in conference, we would not need to compete with each other. It should be possible, for example, to work out a co-ordinated strategy for approaching large funding trusts for grants to support children's evangelism. We could identify places where new work would be most effective. Trusts are reticent about giving grants to work that has no long-term strategy. They would be impressed by such a 'joined up' approach.

Working together, leaders could identify key areas for concern across the country. For example, there are places where nothing at all is happening in any denomination.

Identify where new work would be most effective.

Given impetus from national leaders, such places could be identified as priority areas for resources, training and encouragement. This could prove stimulating and energising to the churches in those areas.

And finally ...

With leaders committed to working together, it would be possible for churches to agree priorities, locally, regionally and nationally. We could know how the ministry at our own church or fellowship complemented and supported the work of our neighbouring church community. Rather than competing against one another, their success would be ours; our struggles would be of importance to them. We would share our celebrations and have a vested interest in praying together.

Is all this possible? Yes it is, but we need leadership for it to happen. We already have committed children's leaders in many local churches, and on the national scene there are gifted, committed people who offer excellent training and promote good practice. But now we need to hear from the national church leaders. They must acknowledge that the church faces a crisis. We need them to gather in common concern and to speak out about children and evangelism. People take notice when they speak.

 Talk about it . . .

- What are the benefits of local churches meeting together?
- How can we ensure that such meetings are creative, helpful, positive experiences?
- How can we encourage members of a variety of churches to listen to one another and to learn from one another?
- What positive ways are there of handling people who have a consistently negative response to new ideas?
- It's great to share resources, but how can we do so without making the recipients feel unimportant and powerless?

 You can continue this discussion by visiting the web on www.chancetochoose.com

Storybox 8
Take the children away!

Residential breaks in a Christian environment can have a great impact on many people, children included. Elm House Centre in Redmire, Yorkshire, is a Christian conference and holiday venue administered by the Jonas Trust. It offers residential respite care and recreation for carers and disadvantaged families. George and Jill Lihou describe its work.

It's valuable to tell the gospel story to a child. It's even more valuable to be able to tell it to the child systematically every day for a week. More rewarding still is to be able to give that child the opportunity to see the gospel lived out by people who are not only telling the story but enjoying great fun with them as well!

We had spent many summers doing just that in Christian camps. These proved to us, beyond doubt, that providing opportunities for children to hear and experience the gospel was well worth it. When this was done in a residential setting, it brought great and long-lasting rewards. Children noticed that Jesus really does make a difference to people, because their leaders lived with them. They noticed how their leaders reacted to provocation and they saw them interact with each other. They saw the fruit of the Spirit as they listened to the story of Jesus. Many children chose to have it growing in their own lives too.

Increasingly after camp each year God was challenging us:

- Why just ten days? Why not extend the season with more permanent accommodation?
- Why only in the summer? Why not provide more opportunities?
- Why not children in the context of whole families?
- Why not make it more widely affordable with self-catering accommodation?

So the Jonas Trust was formed. Jonas was the 'Jesus' character in a 'gospel parallel' story from which many children had benefited at camp. In autumn 1996 the Lord led us to develop Elm House Centre in Wensleydale, Yorkshire – where Wallace and Gromit get their cheese from! This beautiful, rural location is within easy reach of many urban centres. The people from churches in such areas need to get away from the stress and pressures of life.

Our 'permanent tents' became accommodation in a mix of log cabins, cottages and apartments. There is space for games and playgrounds for children. There are meeting rooms and a hall where groups can gather. A well-furnished kitchen enables corporate catering. We have ponies, donkeys, goats and ducks. They all help to provide a completely new experience for the many inner-city children who come to stay.

We have continued our annual camp for ten- to twelve-year-olds. We host a Falcon Camp for children from disadvantaged backgrounds. We offer about thirty weekends a year to churches, enabling them to get away together. They come to Redmire to enjoy fellowship, to get to know one another better, to worship informally and to enjoy the Bible.

Sadly we have seen some visiting churches marginalise the children. They are keen to provide a good programme for the adults, but instead of ensuring an exciting time for their children, they leave them to their own devices. Instead of being affirmed as important members of the church, they have returned home with a memory of being ignored. Instead of discovering the wonder of being part of a dynamic Christian fellowship, they have been bored.

Since our concern is for children, we wanted to change this. So now we offer a children's programme while the adults are meeting. We try to provide a positive Christian experience for them. It's difficult because there's too little time to get to know the children, but we try to design the teaching activities for their particular needs.

With the help of volunteers we offer Christian family holiday weeks with a family service, daytime activities for children and evening sessions for adults. There is also time to enjoy being together as a family, sometimes with grandparents too.

We also incorporate local village children in these activities. We have regular contact with them through our monthly club. We have provided holidays for Romanian orphans and for children from Chernobyl. We would love to welcome others with such special needs.

During the school terms when children are unavailable we are open for individuals and groups whenever space is available. We invite them to come away and discover what God can make possible in their lives. Those who pay full fees enable us to be more generous to others. Those whose needs are greatest are often least able to pay. Our staff is small in order to keep our charges down.

Our vision is growing and developing. There is much more to be done when funds permit. Wait for the next instalment of our story!

9. Reliability Guaranteed
The eternal promises of God

I once knew an elderly woman who kept a 'promise box' at her bedside. As a child, the box fascinated me with its neat, tightly packed scrolls of paper standing side by side, a different Bible promise printed on each one. Tiny tweezers inside the box enabled me to lift out the scroll of my choice. Being allowed to do this was such a treat that when I read one of the promises I felt as if I were choosing a chocolate from a beautiful box.

Promises, promises

Underpinning all our plans and dreams are the big, dependable promises of God. Yes, we have been given minds that think logically through cause and effect – and it is good to use them – but faith helps us take the vitally important next step of believing God's promises. As we consider all the big factors in children's evangelism, it is so important that we bank on the promises of God.

Promises for all time

In the Old Testament, many of God's promises are worded to apply to 'every generation'. The ancient people of God took this to heart. Their psalms encouraged them to absorb the beauty of God's presence. The prophets harangued them to grapple with the foundational truths of their faith. Their leaders wanted them to be clear in their own minds about what God had said and what he had done so that the next generation would hear accurately about God and in their turn have a life-changing of their own.

> Walk about Zion, go round her,
> count her towers,
> consider well her ramparts,
> view her citadels,
> that you may tell of them to the next generation.
> For this God is our God for ever and ever;
> he will be our guide even to the end.
>
> (Psalm 48:12–14)

> I will open my mouth in parables,
> I will utter hidden things, things from of old –
> what we have heard and known,
> what our fathers have told us.
> We will not hide them from their children;
> we will tell the next generation
> the praiseworthy deeds of the Lord,
> his power, and the wonders he has done.
> He decreed statutes for Jacob
> and established the law in Israel,

176

which he commanded our forefathers
to teach their children,
so that the next generation would know them,
even the children yet to be born,
and they in turn would tell their children.
Then they would put their trust in God
and would not forget his deeds
but would keep his commands.

(Psalm 78:2–7)

Promised inheritance

Passages like Deuteronomy 6 and 11 make it clear that the faith of God's people was meant to be handed on. It was not simply for those who had been slaves in Egypt, or those entering Canaan. All the glorious experience and all the harsh reality of being the people of God was to be passed on. As each new generation of children heard about all that had happened, it would be as if they had been there at the time.

Look at Deuteronomy 11:1–7, part of a key passage in which God charges his people with the responsibility of never forgetting what he has done for them. This 'shared memory' was to be a major aspect of their identity as a people. God makes it clear that all adults, regardless of whether or not they are parents, hold responsibility for this transmission.

The same 'shared emphasis' is true of the psalms. They were written for the people to sing, not simply for the priests. There was always the risk that ordinary people would not use the right words, ordinary parents might not hand on their faith in the most appropriate way, but they were still under orders to do so.

That risk has always been there. The gospel was entrusted to a disorganised and unstructured church. Jesus gave his commission to make disciples to a group of unreliable men. A popular description of the situation goes as follows:

A letter from an employment agency to Jesus, circa AD 30

Thank you for submitting the résumés of the twelve men you have picked for managerial positions in your new organisation. All of them have now taken our tests; we have also arranged personal interviews for each of them with our psychologist and vocational aptitude consultant.

It is the staff opinion that most of your nominees are lacking in background, education and vocational aptitude for the type of enterprise you are undertaking. Simon Peter is emotionally unstable and given to fits of temper. Andrew has absolutely no qualities of leadership. The two brothers, James and John, sons of Zebedee, place personal interest above company loyalty. Thomas demonstrates a questioning attitude that would tend to undermine morale. We feel that it is our duty to tell you that Matthew has been blacklisted by the Greater Jerusalem Better Business Bureau. James and John, the sons of Alphaeus and Thaddaeus, definitely have radical leanings and they both registered a high score on the manic-depressive scale.

One of the candidates, however, shows great potential. He is a man of ability and resourcefulness, meets people well, has a keen business mind, and has contacts in high places. He is highly motivated, ambitious and responsible. We recommend Judas Iscariot as your controller and right-hand man. All the other profiles are self-explanatory. We wish you every success in your new venture.[1]

There has always been the risk that God's people would not obey his commandment, or that they would obey it imperfectly. God is prepared to take the risk. He also promises that obedience will bring his blessing.

Promises for the young

God's promises for the young continue through the New Testament. Matthew's accounts of key teachings of Jesus (18:1–14; 19:13–15) help form our mandate for attitudes to children in the church. They are tiny stories in the whole span of the gospel narrative, but their inclusion in Scripture is extraordinarily significant because in the first-century world, children were low-status people. These passages show Jesus welcoming and making promises concerning children. His condemnation of those who prevent children from coming to him is as severe as any he made.

Promises to give us hope

God's promises are for the present and for the future. They are not simply to help lighten today. They are to encourage us as we face a completely unknown future. However intelligent or imaginative we may be, none of us knows what even the next minute will bring into our lives. God's promises give us confidence as we peer through fog into the

---

[1] Quoted in a letter to *The Times Magazine*, 28 July 2001.

future. He promises his presence (Matthew 28:20), his guidance and protection (John 16:13) and his return (John 14:3). And, of course, he promises the glorious reality of heaven.

The glorious reality of heaven?

Promises of blessing

These promises stand as God's unchanging word in our time too. As we face the present national crisis in children's evangelism, we are not on our own. There is no lack of available blessing – God has promised it for his obedient people. There is no lack of power – the Holy Spirit was sent at Pentecost and has never been recalled. God is here among us with power to save. He has made irreversible promises to do so. Nor is there any lack of opportunity: we have plenty of children and the laws of our country leave us free to speak out about our faith. The time is ours!

Promises to bank on ...

We do not need to rely on rolled-up papers in a 'promise box'. We worship the God who is the same today as he was long ago, and he will prove to be the same dependable God in our future. We need to know his promises and to bank on them.

God has made it clear that his promises apply 'from generation to generation'. He has always spoken to his people in their own time. He has also revealed his unchanging character through the Ten Commandments, through his covenants and through Jesus.

He has made it a principle that those who obey him may expect his blessing. Those who disobey must expect judgement.

... but not to presume on

While we trust God's promises, we should never presume that he will fulfil them come what may.

As God's people in the British Isles, we are guilty of taking God's promises for granted. We have been disobedient and not taught the things of God to our children. We have ignored the disappearance of the young from our churches, and have not responded to their loss with remorse and repentance. We have not changed our ways or turned aside from the 'Hezekiah attitude'. We presume that God will still keep his promises. It is as if we have said to ourselves, 'But God always keeps a remnant of his people. There will always be enough left to carry on. It will be all right in my lifetime.'

Judgement

At the time of God's judgement of King Ahab (1 Kings 17), there were many individual people who remained obedient (1 Kings 19:18), but God withheld individual blessing because of national disobedience.

It seems to me that in our society today we are getting on with our own Christian lives, reading our Bibles and saying our prayers, trusting God for personal blessing. But when it comes to handing on the faith to the next generation, there is corporate disobedience.

I am sure we shall continue to experience God's provision for us in our individual situations, as Elijah did – described in these amazing chapters – but we shall only know the full release of God's power, the arrival of the torrential rain (1 Kings 18:45), when there is repentance for this national sin.

Conditions of blessing

Ours is a God of grace. He blesses us in spite of our failures, not because of our successes. But he also yearns for us to obey him because he made us for unclouded relationship with himself. How should we be 'getting in line' with him?

Face the facts

Too many people say that there is nothing new about the present crisis. They are ready to point out the failings of

Sunday schools, giving examples of how children they know have been put off religion by their over-zealous parents. Others take refuge in the belief that this generation of children is unlike any other and they are convinced that it cannot be reached with the gospel. They are wrong. Acknowledging the crisis, rather than evading the challenge, is the first important step to obedience.

Dare to get involved

Many of us may think we are unqualified for working with children – too old, lacking in aptitude, far from ideal. But God tends not to use 'the ideal'. He uses people who are obedient and available. If we are prepared to obey, we shall see what he can do to change the situation. God *will* use us.

The temptation may be to leave things to others. We all have plenty of calls on our time, energy and money. Perhaps it feels that we have little left to spare. But the biblical response to any call from God is, 'Lord, here am I. Send me.'

Until we make that worshipful, full-hearted response to a genuine call from God we shall not know what he can do, or what our role could be. With God we always sign a blank cheque. It takes courage to trust him, to make ourselves available, to be obedient.

True belief

A fundamental challenge remains: to dare to believe fully in evangelism among the young. It calls into question our belief in a living God whose love and mercy continue from generation to generation. It forces us to ask if we look at children with hearts longing that they should know the forgiveness, strength and hope that we have received. Do we have the vision not only for their coming to faith but for their children and their children's children? Do we long for Christian hope not simply for today's children, but for future generations whom we shall never know?

Prayer can turn the tide

God loves to change people – and situations. Working through the Bible, through preaching and in the lives of believers, the Holy Spirit can change heart attitudes. As always, prayer remains an integral part of the process. The Spirit stirs people to pray, and we should pray for this stirring to spread through his people.

How can we encourage the church across the British Isles to pray? Apart from during times of crisis, we tend not to be prayerful people. Will we acknowledge the seriousness of the 'missing children' crisis sufficiently to start to pray? How can we encourage that to happen throughout these islands? Let's encourage five different strands of the church to pray.

Ministers and clergy

What a strong signal it would be to the church if ministers and clergy took the lead in praying for children and evangelism. The message would be clear: work with children is mainstream ministry, not a 'childcare' sideline.

Parents

The pace of family life is relentless. Being a parent is a full-time job – and then some. Asking parents to come together to pray may seem like the final straw. But when parents pray they are putting their trust openly in their own heavenly Father. They are acknowledging that without his help they will fail as parents. When parents pray they show others how important their children are to them. They are expressing their concern for their children to come to know God for themselves and recognising that their family could reveal Jesus to others. Finally, when their parents pray children receive the message of their own value in a new way.

Teachers

I have already encouraged members of the local church to pray for schools in the community; for the children and teachers, regardless of whether or not they are Christians. But given their role and influence, it is also important for Christian teachers to come together to pray. In fact, it is of vital importance to the development of children's evangelism.

It doesn't matter whether teachers meet in small school-based groups or gather together from across a city or region – their prayers are vitally important in the focusing of concern for children to hear the gospel. As they pray, their faith for their schools will grow, their imaginations will be alerted to the potential of the children in their care, and their own lives will become more focused, making them sharpened tools for the Holy Spirit to use. When they pray people will get to hear about it. Prayer is infectious, and their churches, their homes, their friends and family will be affected.

Other adults

There is a whole army of other adults who could, and should, be praying:

- Members of local church policy-making groups.
- Grandparents and godparents.
- Leaders of children's groups and uniformed organisations.
- People who came to faith as children.
- Those who missed out on a Christian upbringing.
- People who are concerned about the lack of children in the church.
- People who have children as friends and neighbours.
- Those who enjoy children's artwork, drama and singing in the church.

Throughout the church there should be a voice of prayer for children. It should express thanks and praise for childhood, and supplication and concern for the lost.

Children

Yes, children can pray for children! When it comes to childhood, children are the only ones with the inside information.

They know what to pray about instinctively, using matter-of-fact and straightforward words. Their faith may make us hesitate, but we do not need to protect them from prayer and we do not need to make excuses for God in case he doesn't answer. God hears the prayers of faith, and children are far more capable of praying in faith than some adults.

Children may, however, need some practical help from adults. For example, adults could prepare, serve and do the clearing up for a children's prayer breakfast, leaving the children free to get on with praying. Or they may need an adult to authorise a lunchtime school group, or to provide a safe meeting place after school. God does not need an adult voice for him to find prayer acceptable. Quite the opposite seems to be true.

Here are some hints for helping any of these groups to keep going over an extended period of time:

- Agree a short list of concerns on which to focus your prayers.
- Spend more time praying about the items on the list than on discussing them.
- Allow people to feel free to use songs, silence and spoken hymns/poetry to help express their thoughts and concerns.
- Pause during the prayer time to ask what people sense God may be saying.
- Always give thanks specifically for answered prayers and keep a record of them.

And finally ...

Prayer is the heart of the life of God's people, and our hearts have grown cold. Many churches have forgotten the excitement of answered prayer. That's why they have lost the hunger for time spent with God in prayer.

Through our intercessions God furthers his purposes for those prayed for, and for the ones who are praying. Our lack of intercession threatens the health of the church.

Let's encourage one another to put time and energy into prayer. Let's resolve to pray for children across our country – children who should be given the chance to choose Jesus!

 Talk about it ...

- What does it mean to trust God in the face of the current crisis in children's evangelism?
- How do we get involved in children's evangelism if there is a lack of whole-church concern?
- How can we keep the right balance between trusting God's promises and taking his judgement seriously?
- It's great to meet regularly to pray. How do we beat the boredom factor and keep those times fresh and invigorating?

 You can continue the discussion by visiting the web on www.chancetochoose.com

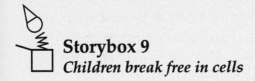

Storybox 9
Children break free in cells

Cell groups make the whole breadth of church life – fellowship,
worship, teaching, pastoral care and outreach – available in small
groups. St John's, Bowling, in Bradford, is one of Britain's pioneer
cell churches. It has children's cells as well as adult ones. Sue Croft
is a member there, and told me how the children's cells work.

Why have children's cells?

We introduced children's cell groups along with adult
groups seven years ago. We believe that God wants to use
children as much as adults to seek and save the lost.
When children were shouting, 'Hosanna to the Son of David'
(Matthew 21:15), Jesus quoted Psalm 8:2 to the indignant
priests: 'From the lips of children and infants you have
ordained praise because of your enemies, to silence the foe
and the avenger.' The children had understood what some
adults hadn't.

In cells, children develop their relationship with God. He
loves this and responds, giving them supernatural gifts.
They then apply their knowledge of Jesus to everyday situations. Within small groups they build closer relationships,

sharing hopes and worries, praying together and supporting each other. They look outwards, praying for non-Christian friends.

Who's involved?

Our children's cell groups cover the under-5s and the 5–11s. Having young children in a cell means they know Jesus from as early an age as possible. They can begin to build relationships with each other. Praying and sharing with one another becomes natural.

When do they meet?

Children's cells have met on Sundays during the latter part of the morning service, but now they meet midweek with their own service on a Sunday.

However, there also needs to be an opportunity for the children to meet outside the cell and with other children. This has involved such things as parties in the park and church, or events led by children's evangelists such as Ishmael and Duggie Dug Dug. Children need such opportunities to invite friends along.

What happens in the cells?

The structure of the cell is similar to that of adult groups. We use the four Ws – Welcome, Worship, Word, Witness (outreach) – but there is an additional element of a craft activity, usually done at the end. This reinforces part of what has been covered during the cell, relating to one of the Ws. It gives children something to take away to remind them of what they have done and to provide a starting point for them to tell others about it. Hence the activity needs to be of the highest quality; something they will want to take away and share with others.

We have used published materials to support what is done in cells, but in the main we have developed our own so that the application is relevant and appropriate. This takes time to prepare, but is worth it.

At times we have also tried to match what the children are doing by addressing the same topic in adult cells. This proved difficult, but did give families opportunity to share more closely.

Who leads the cells?

The adult leader of a children's cell has a complex role as they not only lead one group but are also part of an adult cell. Divided loyalties and expectations can cause frustration unless everyone is aware of the dual role from the outset.

As the numbers have increased, so has the need for leaders. With few adults coming forward, we saw something that should have been obvious: God was calling children to lead their peers in cells. They need to be supported by an adult coach for training and they have adults present at the meeting but the adults do not lead. For example, Julie first asked Jesus into her life when she was three years old. Five years later, she is training to lead a cell group. Children's cell groups, like their adult equivalents, exist to enable members to develop their relationship with God and to share their faith with others. The groups then grow and multiply. Julie's experience reflects the church experience of cell groups: after an initial commitment comes the journey of development and growth.

What next?

This year we have been training these young leaders, and the number of cell groups will increase as peer-led groups develop, giving children in the five to eleven age range an opportunity to be part of midweek cells.

Whatever the organisation, the responsibility is the same. Julie and others like her are encouraged to grow in their relationship with God and become all he wants them to be. The responsibility is awesome, but it's a great privilege.

10. What's Been Going On?

Twelve significant factors for children's evangelism

The context of children's evangelism in the British Isles at the beginning of a new century shows many different influences. Let's look briefly at twelve significant factors, all of which have played a role over the last fifteen years. Each has contributed to present-day thinking and practice.

The Children Act 1989

This important legislation was introduced to raise the standards of work and services with children in England and Wales. (There is equivalent legislation for Scotland and Northern Ireland.) It aims to provide a uniform standard against which all work should be measured. Its official summary states that it is

an Act to reform the law relating to children; to provide for local authority services for children in need and others; to amend the law with respect to children's homes, community homes, voluntary homes and voluntary organisations; to make provision with respect to fostering, child minding and day care for young children and adoption; and for connected purposes.

As far as the local church is concerned, the key issues addressed by the Act include:

- Requirement of basic screening for all volunteers.
- Regulation concerning minimum ratio of adults to children.
- Requirement of basic, appropriate, sanitary provision.
- Restriction of time for a child to be apart from a parent.
- Regulations concerning transport.

This was a significant Act for churches, and many have struggled to comply with its requirements. Denominational headquarters and local social services also provide child-related policy guidelines for local churches. Regional denominational staff as well as national organisations such as the Churches' Child Protection Advisory Service continue to keep churches alert and equipped in this vitally important aspect of their work with children.

Children in the Way

Published in 1998, this report[1] focused on the 'place of children in the church'. Its introduction went on:

---

[1] *Children in the Way* (National Society/Church House Publishing, 1988).

This means challenging those who make decisions and those who work with children's groups. We want them to acknowledge once more the responsibility which all adults have to share their faith with the children of the church and to go out to children and families outside the church. We believe that this is to be accomplished by developing relationships between people of all ages within the church, and between church people and children and families outside the church.

The report placed a major emphasis on the 'pilgrim model' of being church and of sharing faith. The title's double meaning prepares the reader for this approach. It challenges those who consider that children get in the way, and illustrates the idea of the child as a fellow-pilgrim.

Children in the Way challenged all those who make decisions about children and all those involved in the hands-on work with children in churches. It was realistic in its approach and provided many examples of good practice. Its discussion was earthed in the authentic and sometimes surprising comments made by children themselves.

All God's Children?

Subtitled 'Children's evangelism in crisis', this report[2] appeared in 1991, and I was a member of the working party. Our aim was to 'alert the churches to the seriousness of the situation, suggest some of the theological and pastoral issues

---

[2] *All God's Children?* (National Society/Church House Publishing, 1991).

and indicate considerations that need to be taken in mind as the churches attempt to move forward'.

Our introduction went on to say that as a result of our research, we had come to feel that we had a vision and a burden to share with the churches. Our report was 'unashamedly coloured' by the sense of urgency we felt after two years of considering the subject. We underlined the fact that in the 1990s only fifteen children out of every 100 had any direct contact with a Christian church. The report argued for new priorities in the church in order to communicate the gospel to the millions of children who faced adult life without any awareness of a God who loved them. It highlighted the false gospels and values that contemporary society was offering children. It called for the church to take children seriously and to develop a radical new strategy for children's work and evangelism. It was hard-hitting and was 'written by an ecumenical working party in the belief that nothing less than a concerted effort will meet the challenge of helping all our children to realise that they are indeed All God's Children'.

Bishop Gavin Reid, formerly Bishop of Maidstone, was the member of the working party who provided the necessary editorial skills. He told me recently:

In January 2001 the Archbishop of Canterbury appointed an Officer for Evangelism among Children to work with the Archbishops' Council Boards of Mission and Education with a brief to stimulate evangelistic outreach to children throughout the Church of England. That move came close on the heels of a readiness of the Archbishops of York and Canterbury to commend your work, Penny, which also aims to raise the profile of this critical area of mission.

The appointment of the Archbishop's Officer is the first high-level response to the publication of *All God's Children* ten years previously. (The General Synod debated the report in November 1991, and it was accepted by a near unanimous vote.) Some of us who were involved in writing the report have found the apparent inactivity of the past ten years almost unbearable. Why, seemingly, has so little taken place? Do we have a church that has no heart for children?

I think we get a better perspective on this if we ask what has happened to any of the other dozens of reports that the General Synod and other bodies have commended to the church over the last ten years. The truth is that reports achieve very little. The gap between the central 'talkers' of the church – and this is true across all the denominations – and the local 'doers' and worshippers is far bigger than all our talk of representative government would suggest.

But I feel more hopeful of progress now than at any time. The Archbishop's imaginative appointment is, from the point of view of the Church of England, a hopeful one. Of course one person can only do so much, but the symbolic linking of this agenda to the leaders of the Church of England is tremendous. When David Hope, Archbishop of York, was kind enough to make some comments on my recent retirement from the affairs of the General Synod, he described *All God's Children* as a 'groundbreaking' report on which more needed to be done.

Both the Lambeth Conference in 1998 and now the Archbishops' Council have identified evangelism among children as a major priority. That is an improvement on the talk of ten years ago. But the problem remains that not much gets across the big gap between the people who talk in synods and councils and the people in our pews and local church committees. We need to reach local congregations not only with the vision for children's evangelism, but also with practical resources.

The Tide Is Running Out

Dr Peter Brierley's English Church Attendance Survey appeared in 2000.[3] This comprehensive survey of Sunday attendance in churches of all denominations showed an accelerating decline in the average number of churchgoers and indicated that many of these were children. Dr Brierley noted that this 'loss' was the equivalent of the disappearance of 1,000 children per week from Sunday attendance. The report called for close attention to be given to this area of ministry: 'It was because information received was disregarded, it was too late to save the Titanic when eventually the lookout cried: "Ice ahead!"'

Here are some snapshots from the report:

- 41 per cent of churches across the denominations have no children under three years of age.

---

[3] *The Tide Is Running Out* (Christian Research, 2000).

- 70 per cent of church attenders come to faith by the age of twenty.
- Church attendance has dropped by one million in nine years. Half of that decline is from the under-fifteen age group.

Brierley urges: 'Focus urgently on children. Understand their technological world. Work more with schools where contact with most of the nation's children is guaranteed.'

Research

The church owes a considerable debt of gratitude to people like Leslie Francis, Jeff Astley and David Lankshear, whose scholarly research over the years has provided information the church has needed to hear. Throughout these years when there has been such a loss of children from the church, this reliable research has been our 'look out' call. The warnings have been given, but it seems that the advice has been largely ignored.

Among other things their research has produced:

- *The Child in the Church* (British Council of Churches, 1976).
- *How Faith Grows* (National Society/Church House Publishing, 1991) – faith development and Christian education.
- *In the Evangelical Way* (National Society, 1995) – children and young people in evangelical churches.
- *In the Catholic Way* (National Society, 1995) – children and young people in Anglo-catholic parishes.
- 'The impact of children's work on village church life' (*Spectrum* 21, 1992).
- 'Do small churches hold a future for children and young people?' (*Modern Churchman* 33, 1991).

The cell-church model

In recent years the 'cell' way of being church has hit the headlines. Seen by many larger churches as a new way forward, this approach seeks to structure the main life of the church primarily through small groups. These groups are intended to be more than supportive, pastoral-care-focused home groups. Cell groups aim for growth through evangelism. It is important that this model of church does not marginalise children. Daphne Kirk is a leader at Ely Christian Fellowship, and she has given a lot of thought to the inter-generational possibilities of cell church. Many churches are restructuring in this way and introducing children to the cell groups.

The church of St Michael-le-Belfrey in York has cell groups for children. Church member Joy Martin describes how they include the key cell-church features of Welcome, Worship, Word and Witness:

The Welcome is always something fun, often including a craft, as this is a great excuse for leaders to chat to children. Also games help to use up energy and bind the group together. Worship varies each week, but we have been experimenting with lots of different types of worship. We have been amazed how lying on the floor listening to Celtic music has helped these children to meet with God. But we also use shouting, guitars, CDs . . . in fact anything which will help our children to focus on God.

With these age groups the Word section is interactive. Our young leaders are great at dressing up as Bible characters, and puppets seem to capture our young people's imagination. Variety and interaction seem to be the keys.

The Word is then applied in cells. These are leader-led in the younger age groups but we are always looking out for young people who want to lead and they are given the opportunity for part of the cell time . . . Cell time is always about applying the Word and always includes praying for each other. This leads naturally into the Witness section where friends are prayed for.[4]

---

[4] *Generation 2 Generation*, Issue 12.

The Kidz Klub model

Based in Brooklyn, New York, Metro Ministries' Bill Wilson has been reaching children outside the church for the last eighteen years. In one week, Metro's Kidz Klub can reach up to 20,000 children, bussed in from surrounding needy areas.

Recent years have seen the successful development of this model in Britain. Turn to Storybox 3 ('Tough rules for tough kids') to learn more about how Kidz Klub is working in an area of urban deprivation.

Midweek ministry

The last ten years have brought a challenge to the church's traditional Sunday school approach to children's ministry. Many churches have felt forced to explore midweek groups. Several factors have contributed to this new approach:

- Far-flung families – 'Sunday is when we visit Grandma in Carlisle'.
- The difficulty of providing leadership for children's groups on Sunday.
- Many children have sport/music/drama commitments on Sunday.
- The growing culture of 'weekends away'.
- Many see Sunday as a 'family day' for personal pursuits.
- Where there is a high percentage of 'latch-key kids',

weekday after-school provision is seen as a community service.

Alan Charter, head of Scripture Union's Missions Department, comments:

> The increasing shift to midweek activity to reach and disciple children is a welcome step in the right direction. It is great to see people adopting new models of reaching and discipling children. However, it is not time to sit back and pat ourselves on the back. The speed at which society changes by far outpaces that at which the church responds to change. We must both pray and take action if we are to see this spiritually needy generation of children reached with the good news of Jesus. I believe this is by far the most important strategy any church can develop to see the kingdom of God grow.

Way Ahead

Produced under the leadership of Lord Dearing and sub-titled 'Church of England Schools in the New Millennium', this is the first major inquiry into the subject for more than fifteen years.[5] It offers an exciting vision for their future. The report argues that church schools must be distinctively Christian institutions, providing good education to children from all backgrounds. In setting out its recommendations, the review group aims to give substance to the resolution of

---

[5] *Way Ahead – Church of England Schools in the New Millennium* (Church House Publishing, 2001).

the Church of England's General Synod that inspired its work: 'Church schools stand at the centre of the Church's mission to the nation.'

It is worth looking at the report's challenging executive summary.

1. The General Synod and the Archbishops' Council have identified Church schools as standing at the centre of the Church's mission to the nation. Our work over the last eighteen months has confirmed the crucial importance of Church schools to the whole mission of the Church to children and young people, and indeed to the long-term well-being of the Church of England.

2. The Church's mission can only be discharged through Church schools if there is a sufficiency of these schools across the land. We found very large variations in provision between one diocese and another, and in particular in contrast to the Roman Catholic Church – small provision of secondary schools in relation to primary places. This leads to a growing imbalance between the ability of many Church secondary schools to offer places and the parental demand for them. A recent survey of some eighty Church of England secondary schools showed that for every 100 places there were 160 applications. We therefore recommend that over the next seven to eight years the Church seeks, in partnership with local authorities, to provide whether through additional Church secondary schools or the expansion of existing schools the equivalent of an extra 100 Church secondary schools.

3. We note that primary school provision is also varied, and recommend that dioceses should strengthen their provision where it is particularly sparse.

4. To facilitate the proposed expansion, we recommend national fundraising to assist dioceses, and that the objective should be to raise £25 million over seven years.

5. Expansion of provision is not enough. To be at the heart of the Church's mission, Church schools must be distinctively Christian and we make recommendations to secure best practice.

6. Nor can Church schools be fully engaged in the Church's mission at parish level unless they are in close partnership with the worshipping community, and we make a range of practical recommendations to develop this partnership.

7. We welcome action by recent Governments to bring the Church into partnership in the provision of schools and thereby widen parental choice. Central to our thinking is the growing partnership between diocesan and local education authorities, and we make recommendations on the way this partnership can develop.

8. No factor will be more important in determining the future of Church schools than the Church's ability to recruit Christian teachers and develop heads and deputy heads to provide the excellent leadership that will be needed in the additional secondary schools we propose. This will be crucial if, as we recommend, the Church should be especially concerned to serve areas of great economic and social need. We make recommendations accordingly, and on encouraging the vocation to teach.

9. We support an ecumenical approach to new schools, and make recommendations for strengthening the links between

maintained Church schools and independent schools that have an Anglican foundation, which we see as an important part of the family of Church schools.

10. We make recommendations for the training of clergy, primarily at the post-ordination stage, to equip them to be both effective and welcome in schools.

11. In our final chapter, we turn to the Church colleges of higher education where we make recommendations to secure and enhance their Christian distinctiveness, and to secure their long-term future.

12. As a general theme throughout our report, we urge all elements in the Church community to look afresh at the way they work together, for in a community of purpose the work of the Church will be enhanced. We have in mind in particular the relationship between the parish and the Church school; the working relationships between the Church colleges, one with another, and their relationships with dioceses and schools.

13. In conclusion, we have a clear view that this is a time of opportunity for the Church, when there is much goodwill towards Church schools both at the national level from main political parties and at the local level, from many parents, and encouragement to increase the provision of Church schools. Our report is offered as a contribution to developing a way ahead. We make a full statement of our recommendations at the end of our report.

Increase in full-time children's workers

Recent years have seen many churches employing full- or part-time workers for teenagers and children. Claire Lea is Executive Director of AMAZE, a professional body for Christian youth and children's workers. I asked her to comment on the current scene.

Concern about the number of young people leaving the church has resulted in an increasing desire to spend money on employing youth workers. Similarly, as churches have lost touch with young people they have also needed to employ someone who can communicate with young people.

We are now beginning to see the same thing happen with children. *Turning the Tide* has focused attention on the children leaving the church, so now churches are beginning to see the need to spend money on employing children's workers. The pay is low. Children's work is perceived to be lower in value than other forms of church work. This is related to the value currently given to children in the church.

My perception is that many in church work (not only youth and children's work) put in excessive hours because they are 'doing it for the Lord'. They have to work the long hours to feel comfortable alongside members of the congregation who work long hours and then volunteer to do children's work in their 'spare' time.

They also have ministers as line managers who generally are not good at setting boundaries and balancing work/ministry with other activities. There is little teaching on the theology of work and all church workers (and their families and friends) suffer as a consequence.

There's a lack of contracts and formal arrangements. ('Well, this is a church agreement and we can rely on each other's word!')

Children's work is generally poorly supported. It's difficult to get volunteers, maybe because the fruits of your labours may not be seen for a number of years, maybe because the importance/value of children in the church is not recognised. Or maybe it is because generally people are busier and lives are more stressful. Smaller congregations mean fewer people doing more work.

When someone is paid to do the work, forward planning is often forgotten in the relief of someone to cope with the 'now'. This means that leaders can ignore the possibility that the work might grow and need more resources in the future.

Growth of training courses

Recent years have seen the development of an encouraging number of options for those wanting to increase their knowledge of children and evangelism. For those pursuing full-time posts, there is the additional advantage of completing a course with national recognition. Here are some snapshots of courses currently on offer.

Cliff College – Diploma Course in Children's Evangelism and Nurture

This course has been developed as a joint venture between Scripture Union and Cliff College. The diploma is available to all those who are committed to children and the gospel. Admission is based upon perceived potential, qualities of character and Christian conviction, assessed through references and interview at the college. The main criterion, however, is a conviction to reach children for Christ and disciple them in their faith.

The course can be undertaken on its own, but also offers a progression between the certificate level and BA (Hons) in Biblical and Evangelistic Ministry. It is run over two years (part time) and involves three one-week modules per year, one in each term; evangelistic skills workshops; placements and mission activity. The diploma is examined by assignments, course work and dissertation. The teaching blocks include: The Place of Children in God's Kingdom; The Law and the Child; Child Development; Children and Spirituality; Discipleship; Communicating with Children; Leadership and Management Issues and Skills.

Writing as the first students of the course graduated in summer 2001, Course Leader Ian White commented:

For me the great excitement of the CEN course is to see children's workers – the often forgotten or sidelined workers of the church – growing in knowledge, skill and confidence. The church of the future is going to need children's workers who are able to tackle the theological issues of contemporary childhood, and offer a lead to the church in terms of biblical understanding and practice. Models of children's work and outreach will have to change in order to reconnect with the huge numbers of children who have no understanding of living Christian faith – it's amazing to see the skills and talents of the students grow within the course. But maybe above all, the course gives a greater confidence to children's evangelists and to their particular calling and task. Their work is significant, their calling essential, and their task increasingly important to the future life of the church.

The excitement comes with the realisation that [the desire for more] children's evangelists has led to a respected and, I believe, influential course, whose graduates will make a huge impact in reaching children and making Jesus known to them across this country and beyond.

Oak Hill College – Youth and Children's Ministry Course

This course began in the autumn of 2001. It offers:

- Confidence in handling God's word with children and young people.
- Skill in providing pastoral care.
- Maturity to encourage children and young people to relate to the entire body of Christ rather than being an isolated group within the local church.
- Leadership and training skills, coupled with sensitivity and respect for volunteer co-workers.
- Creativity in devising programmes for church-based youth or children's work.
- Learning to work for the minister and as a partner in the leadership of the church.

The course aims to help those coming to it with a strong youth/teenager bias to be educated and equipped to work confidently with children.

London Bible College – Children's Ministry Course

This course provides teaching on using the Bible with children and an introduction to child and faith development. In the second year, students study current trends in all-age worship and children's services. All of this is underpinned by knowledge of the demands and recommendations of the Children Act and also by the resources available to use in the ministry.

The Schools Work Course equips students to communicate the Christian faith in primary and secondary schools. It explores current issues in education and looks at the specific contribution that can be made by the Christian visitor to the life of the school through worship, lessons and other church school links.

Leading Children – Distance Learning Course

This course helps to give understanding of the world of the modern child. It helps the reader to develop the attitudes and skills that are necessary for successful and confident leadership. The course can be used on its own as the reader absorbs the material. Alternatively it can be used in a group with someone who has already gone through the course acting as group leader/trainer. There is also the opportunity to buy into tutor help as the student goes through the course so that assignments are marked and accreditation given. *Leading Children* is not solely about evangelism but it puts that issue firmly in the centre of the need for healthy and thriving children's ministry in the local church. Please contact Kingsway's Children's Ministry department for further details on 01323 437748.

Scripture Union — Reaching Children

This annual week-long training course is for anyone wishing to devote a week to thinking through the principles and practice of evangelism with children. It aims to resource, challenge and help them, whatever their role. Over the years it has attracted those in church leadership and those in, or considering joining, full-time children's work. It has also welcomed those at the 'coalface' of church-based outreach to children.

Paul Godfrey, Children's Work Advisor for Chelmsford Diocese, helped to launch and staff the course. He says:

> We believe as part of our calling as evangelists and our concern for children, we have a responsibility to develop God's people in the ministry of child evangelism and to share the accumulated experience of Scripture Union from over the years.
>
> We recognise God's view of a child as a whole person, not just as a 'soul to be saved'; we observe the need of children in today's society, so the course seeks to help delegates to understand evangelism in the context of the 'whole child', including child and faith development. We also cover legislative and ethical requirements of working with children.
>
> We believe that an intensive training course is particularly effective in bringing people together from a variety of backgrounds, which facilitates shared learning and affirmation, providing the opportunity to build on the work being done from one session or day to another; and giving space and time to learn and reflect away from one's normal context.
>
> Workshops seek to develop practical skills, but the emphasis of the week remains on 'why' so that delegates have a firmer

212

base on which to decide 'what' and 'how'. We usually include a visit to reflect on work with real children, either in school or in outreach activities. Bible studies and teaching sessions are planned to use a variety of presentational and participative methods. We seek where possible to model good practice that is transferable to other ministry settings.

The Kingsway conferences

From January 1998 Kingsway have provided annual conferences and regional training days for children's leaders. The conferences have attracted between 1,000 and 2,500 delegates each time.

The weekend conferences have included opportunities

- to see a wealth of resources in the exhibition;
- to gain vision and spiritual strength through plenary teaching and worship;
- to be specifically resourced and enabled through workshops and seminars.

The conferences have gained an international flavour with twelve countries being represented at Eastbourne in January 2001.

The training days have attracted between 200 and 300 delegates, with numbers often restricted solely by size of venue.

Obviously events of this size are not solely about children's evangelism. But their emphasis is on growth of the church and on children.

And finally ...

These are exciting years to be around children. Much of what has been listed in this chapter aims to equip people to raise the standard of the work they do with children in and through the church.

Good work is being done. Children are making good relationships with Christians and some of them are finding that this leads them to a relationship with Jesus. There are churches that have thriving children's provision, and this ministry can lead them into healthy children's evangelism.

But it is not enough. It has not been enough to stop the flow of children out of the church. It is not proving enough to reach the millions who were never there.

Don't feel depressed. Flick back to Chapter 2 and focus on the motivation and solution for children's evangelism: Jesus Christ.

Useful contacts

Agencies

AMAZE
PO Box 5898
Hinckley LE10 2YX
Tel: 0121 503 0824
www.amaze.org.uk

Churches' Child Protection Advisory Service (CCPAS)
PO Box 133
Swanley
Kent BR8 7UQ
Tel: 0845 1204550
www.ccpas.org.uk

Cell church

For information about the cell church scene contact Cell
Church UK. www.cellchurch.co.uk

Colleges and training

Children's Ministry
Lottbridge Drove
Eastbourne BN23 6NT
Tel: 01323 437748
www.childrensministry.co.uk

Cliff College
Calver
Hope Valley
Sheffield S32 3XG
Tel: 01246 582321
www.cliffcollege.org

London Bible College
Green Lane
Northwood HA6 2UW
Tel: 01923 456000
www.londonbiblecollege.ac.uk

Oak Hill College
Chase Side
Southgate
London N14 4PS
Tel: 0208 449 0467
www.oakhill.ac.uk

Scripture Union
207–209 Queensway
Bletchley
Milton Keynes MK2 2EB
Tel: 01908 856111
www.scriptureunion.org.uk

Storybox 10
Build God's kingdom, not your empire

*Andy Mason is the youth and children's worker at St James',
Poole. He also helps at a Crusaders after-school club across town.
Crusaders has grown, but his church has not benefited! Does it
matter? Andy thinks not, and explains why. Here is an important
lesson about churches working together.*

I'm petrified of ministers, youth workers and anyone
involved in leading children's work! There you are, minding
your own business, and they smile at you, put their arm
around your shoulder, and ask a favour. But not just any
favour – it's always a big one!

Such was the case with the Crusader group. Karen is the
youth and children's worker from a church on the other side
of town. She was asking for help with an inter-church
Crusader after-school club. 'Yeah, I'll help,' I heard myself
say. I'm a mug at times.

It was a brave experiment. The school was not very sym-
pathetic to Christian things, so it was a gamble. Would children want to stay at school for another hour and fifteen
minutes? And would the local churches see this work as of
equal value to what they did on their premises? After all,

217

churches often have this strange notion that something is valid only if it happens in their building.

The concept of going where the people are is very much how Jesus operated. In this case, we went to their school. Yet often we expect children to come to us. We need to go to them for a change.

There were about eleven children, all under eight, and a few leaders at the first meeting. There also seemed to be an abundance of glue and squash in an over-sized hall with hideous 1970s curtains. As I walked in I thought, 'What have I let myself in for? Why did I say I'd help?'

I soon found out. They were struggling for leaders and just by being there I was helping them meet their legal requirement for children-to-adult ratios – we had enough to keep going. The children enjoyed coming so much that the group began to grow. We finally had to introduce a waiting list.

Some of the early teaching sessions were hard work. We made sure that we put as much effort into the teaching as we did into the games or craft sessions.

John was one of the leaders. He is a youth and children's worker from a neighbouring church. One day John was teaching the parable of the sower. He was telling the children about the different types of soil. Emma put her hand up and said loudly, 'I want to be like the good soil!' At once there was bedlam. Half the kids there called out, 'Yeah, so do I!' It was excellent.

As our numbers have grown we have also seen many of the children move closer to Jesus. Some of them have met him for the first time. We make no high-pressure appeals. We simply tell the children about Jesus, week in week out. God does the rest.

Quite a few of the children have strengthened their links with one of the nearby churches. How many children from the group now come to the church where I work? None whatsoever! The truth is that God wants us to build his kingdom rather than our own little empires. If I hadn't helped out, the group might not have happened. Some of the children would not have become Christians. Others would not have gone deeper in their faith. Just being an extra pair of hands can make the difference between a group happening or not. I've seen God work miraculously in the lives of around thirty children, and it started by rather reluctantly doing a favour for a friend from another church.

It is hardly a radical concept! It's simply Christians from different churches working together to teach children about Jesus. What a shame that it's seldom done! Perhaps you could get started by having coffee with the person who co-ordinates children's work at your neighbouring church. See how they feel about getting involved, and take it from there.

As for schools work, I suggest you take a letter of introduction from your minister to the head of the local school, and ask how you can get involved. Maybe offer to come in to do an assembly or RE lesson. Or perhaps you could offer to help run a lunchtime or after-school club.

The secret of our success is simple:

- We took the risk.
- We worked together.
- We made the effort.
- We kept going.
- God did the rest!

CPAS Church Pastoral Aid Society

CPAS is an Anglican mission agency working across the United Kingdom and the Republic of Ireland to provide a wealth of resources for leaders of local churches.

Our vision is of the local church as a nurturing community evangelising people of all ages. With this in mind, CPAS resources churches for evangelism through consultancy, leadership training and high quality resource material.

CPAS is funded almost entirely through voluntary donations. Contact us for more information on:

Tel: 01926 458458
Email: info@cpas.org.uk
www.cpas.org.uk

CPAS children's evangelism initiative

Labelled 'A Heart for Children' and led by Penny Frank, this important initiative aims to raise the profile of children's evangelism both nationally and at local church level. The aim is simple: to help the church respond positively – and urgently – to the current 'missing children' crisis.

Contact us for more information on:

CPAS
Athena Drive
Tachbrook Park
Warwick CV34 6NG
Tel: 01926 458488
Email: heart@cpas.org.uk
www.chancetochoose.com

A company limited by guarantee.
Registered charity no. 1007820

Children's Ministry Teaching Programme

- Do you want to see children develop a personal relationship with Jesus?

- Do you want teaching sessions that are fun, biblical, evangelical and interactive?

- Would you like children to enjoy age-appropriate activities as they learn about God?

If you've said YES to any of these questions, you need the Children's Ministry Teaching Programme.

The Children's Ministry Teaching Programme provides four leader's guides covering ages from under 3 to 13+; KidZone activity books for children aged 5-7, 7-9 and 9-11; MiniKidz and KidZone craft books for children aged 3-5 and 5-9, a magazine for those over 11; a CD of music and stories; and FamilyZone with song words, ideas for all-age worship and parents' letters.

**For more information visit our web site
www.childrensministry.co.uk**

Reclaiming a Generation
Children – today's church, tomorrow's leaders

by Ishmael

From the author's Introduction:

'I have written this book because I believe it is time to re-evaluate our many traditions, and as we do so, I pray that it will make us more understanding of what the Bible says is expected of our children.

Before you make up your mind to agree or disagree, just look outside your window and ask yourself honestly how the thousands of lost little ones around you will ever get to know Jesus, or get to love the church, if we just stay as we are for the next two thousand years.'